Funky Little Flower Farm

Augustus Jenkins Farmer

Foreword by Richard Olsen, Ph.D.

Independently published in 2019

Book design by Todd Beasley

Illustrations by Cait Maloney Creative, Illustration & Design

Photography credits:
Ezra Barrett: on pages 31 and 93
Patrick Biestman of Acuity Photography: cover and on
pages 22, 38, 44, 49, 51, 67, 68, and 103
Carolyn Cloe: on page 19
Hunter Desportes: on page 63
Jenks Farmer: on pages 12, 15, 20, 23, 26, 27, 30, 34, 38, 42, 43, 45, 54,
55, 57, 59, 60, 64, 74, 80, 83, 86, 95, and 96
Tom Hall: on pages 77 and 89
Lonnie Webster: on pages 5, 7, 14, 37, 48, 52, and 99

Development and Content Editing by Kevin Sharpe / artisancg.net
Copyediting by Margaret O'Shea

ISBN: 9781686213212

To all the people who encourage and push and make me write, thank you.

To my parents who saved this farm from a state of ruin, thank you.

To all the generations of people who came before, free and enslaved, who have ever nurtured this red dirt farm, thank you. You have inspired a responsibility toward stewardship in me and a duty to pass it along to the next generation so they can build an even better world.

Table of Contents

Foreword

Richard Olsen, Ph.D.

Director of The United States National Arboretum

When I first met Jenks Farmer, he was fresh out of graduate school and I was an undergraduate. He had been recently charged with building a brand new botanical garden, the first in the warm part of Zone 8, in Columbia, South Carolina. I was a sophomore at North Carolina State in Raleigh, where my favorite professor, J.C. Raulston, was planting and promoting his young arboretum. J.C. was famous for his generosity with plants, his time, and his home. To promote and share horticulture in the Raleigh area, J.C. had turned his award-winning urban loft into a crash pad and social forum for plants people visiting the horticultural mecca that he helped create in Raleigh. Jenks, always a believer in mentorship, visited often to soak up friendship, knowledge, and truckloads of plants from J.C.

BUILT BEFORE 1900, THE RENOVATED BARN NOW SERVES MODERN
NEEDS WHILE HONORING ORIGINAL STYLES AND MATERIALS.

The idea of a quasi-communal home was an effective and fun model for the cross pollination of horticultural minds. Jenks jumped on board and followed suit. As his team developed Riverbanks Botanical Garden, his house also became a crash pad for horticulture professionals and students. I saw my first towering agave flower-spike at Jenks's house during a boiled peanut party for the crew of a fledgling Massachusetts arboretum. I also recall sleeping on his screened porch through a hot August night—his broken air conditioner had turned the inside of the house into a broiler. And as with J.C., Jenks was mentoring young horticulturists like me. In fact, my first professional lecture was the result of his invitation to present at Riverbanks to our peers at a professional public gardens meeting.

As the designer and horticulturist of Riverbanks, Jenks mostly had dirty hands and became a true plantsman. As a curator, he defined plant accessions, plant records, and all staff positions—insisting on building a strong internship program. Throughout his twenty-five-year career, he's built stimulating internship programs for students of horticulture, landscape architecture, and permaculture programs that have helped many students find their way. He's still doing both today, keeping his hands dirty and helping young people find their path.

This book about Jenks's unique lily farm is firmly rooted in the horticulture of Zone 8, the place our mutual mentor J.C. often referred to as "the orphan zone of horticulture." It's a different world with different soils and frost dates, long hot nights, and awesome plant growth. Plants behave differently there than they do just up the road in Raleigh. Zone 8 is a sliver of climate and land, so horticulture literature is limited for this zone. Times are changing though. Population is booming in Zone 8, and now these residents need serious gardening knowledge. This book offers details about plants and gardening in this climate. In its pages, Jenks presents lessons and plant profiles through stories that can speak to and teach gardeners of any age.

Jenks loves plants on so many levels: how they please us, feed us, and connect us to each other, to history and to the future. In *Funky Little Flower Farm,* Jenks writes with colorful, lyrical words to help us understand his journey and facilitate our own connections with gardens. He doesn't hold back. This is Jenks's story of growing up, his own *Catcher in the Rye,* if you will. It's also the story of how he turned a tired family farm into a dynamic and robust cottage industry without relying on huge capital investments and sometimes even going against conventional wisdom. He writes with a much needed shot of authenticity that deepens our perspectives, breaking through the all too common superficialities of the present. But as we all know, that's Jenks's style. As you take in the stories and images from the pages of this book, you'll come to understand in a very poignant way how to become a gardener in the Deep South.

———

TODAY THE OLD SMOKE HOUSE HAS A NEW LIFE AS A
COLORFUL TOOL SHED.

Introduction

Plants connect. They connect us to the earth and to each other, to our past and to generations yet to come.

When I put my hands on a turnip—any turnip, anywhere—I'm immediately connected, transported to the little farm I grew up on, feeling our sandy, dark farm soil, smelling Momma's greens on the stove, and sitting on Daddy's '67 Dodge pick-up—the one with the wide tailgate, that we sold turnips off of at the farmers market. I can even hear Daddy telling stories to some stranger and making change for a dollar, out loud to teach me how.

Selling turnips off a tailgate. It's a country-song cliché. It's also an expression of a tenet of small farms: grow, nurture, eat, and make some money. This was an endeavor my parents planned for me, equivalent to setting up a lemonade stand. Momma knew it would teach basic financial skills. Daddy knew it would engage me in farming. Around Memorial Day, we'd plow a special row, Jenks's turnip row. We'd nurture the tiny seedlings, water, and compost through fall. On a chilly Friday afternoon in October, we'd start pulling, washing, and bundling greens and purple-topped roots for Saturday morning sales. While that turnip story makes me smile today, the military precision of farm plantings—long, straight rows of crops with the earth hoed clean in between—felt too restrictive back then. To a creative, gay teenager, it was oppressive in many ways. I ran so far away from the farm that even in my career of garden design, I rejected straight lines and made gardens with bold, flowing curves and wild, intermingled plantings.

This book is about coming back home to the farm. Same dirt, same rows, same old barns. But today the farm has a new chic. And a new ethic. I came home with a husband, Tom, and a risky business plan to grow and produce a new crop, flower bulbs, specifically the big, storied bulbs of crinum lilies. Today this farm is comfortable for lots of people. It's a pair of old jeans, a story you like to tell over and over, a song that makes you sing along. At first glance, the old-fashioned farmstead seems simple and sweet. But looking deeper, one sees that a combination of technology and seemingly antiquated farming systems created a cutting-edge nursery that has become a leader, an example of how horticulture can build good soil, good plants, good flowers, food, and a balanced life.

This book is my attempt to share not just my own stories, but also the idea that plants are a medium we can use to learn about and connect to the past. And then pass our lessons on to coming generations.

There are twenty-four stories about this little flower farm in this book, and they fall into two categories.

The first category of story is what I call the sekki moment. It pays homage to the Japanese Sekki calendar, a way of recognizing seasons by natural occurrences, like the first budding of cherry trees or the last leaf falling from full-moon maples. Tom's mother came to America from Japan with her army husband and was cut off from the world she'd known. Hearing stories about how she kept connections to home through flowers and food made me more aware of this lovely, traditional way of marking the passing of seasons. In my Southern sekki essays, certain plants coming into flower or fruit tell me that a month is coming or passing.

The second category of story addresses work that we do each month on the lily farm. These stories reveal lessons about growing plants in our Deep South climate. Like good southerners must, I include healthy doses of nostalgia and a cast of odd characters—real people who come as interns, friends, and yes, a nutty great-aunt, too. While each work story is based on our field work, you can easily translate the lessons to your own home gardening.

Each essay stands alone. But if you read from start to finish, you'll be able to follow several overarching stories. One is about building a small business on a shoestring and without a grand plan. Then there's the coming-of-age story with farm-boy crushes, AIDS, rattlesnakes, and strategic plans. The most important story deals with imagining a better world and setting about to make it a reality.

When all is said and done, we must look back to see the successes and the mistakes of previous generations. We must look inward to understand our own journey, acknowledge our own fears. And we must look forward to pass along our discovered wisdom to the next generation. I hope I do that—even just a little—in these pages. I hope I'm able to help you make connections to your own world through these simple stories. I hope you're inspired to tell your own stories, too. If we all live our connected lives honestly and tell our stories honestly, then we will honor our elders and our own journeys while nurturing the dignity and responsibility of the next generation. With old wisdom and new tools, they'll build better dirt, grow healthier plants, and make a more beautiful world.

Jenks

Weasa

Interns

Momma

Tom

Farm Crew

Momma's Japanese winter flowering apricot
brightens gray January days.

Holding Their Breath

Fat buds of *Prunus mume* wait for the warmer days of winter. Starting around the turn of the year, I eagerly wait for both buds and warmth. Every cold gray day, the bulging buds stand out, puffed up like they're holding their breath along with me. We're all waiting.

Then one lovely day the sun comes out. It's the kind of day that lets me pretend for a few hours that winter is gone. The dogs bask in the sunshine on the dry grass. And then I'll hear it. For a moment I've forgotten that I'm waiting and I think, "What's that noise?" The quiet winter air amplifies the buzzing. Another moment and I think that it may be a swarm of bees though that's not likely this early in winter. But, yeah, it's definitely bees. Then I get a whiff of something. Big Red chewing gum. Tuned senses have told the bees and me the winter-flowering apricot finally has unfurled. Long before I see it, I already have heard it, smelled it. Then I see it—a cloud of pink flowers surrounded by a bronze aura of bees. Those flashes of bees lit by the sun, those languid dogs, and me—we love the first day the mume flowers bloom. It signals the start of a new cycle on the farm. We shift from waiting to working toward spring.

There are four people on today's crew: Tom, Ryan, Maria, and me. We head out to work all bundled up. We men try to work quietly and focus attentively on our work, but Maria chatters and laughs. She's always upbeat, always has a fun outlook on life. The donkey brays and she laughs. A shovel snaps and she laughs. Between Maria, the rising sun, and our physical work, we warm up. We're not just digging but excavating—crinum bulbs grow really deep. No tractors or tilling here, though we sometimes wish there were. This kind of manual labor takes hard work and dedication, but also observation and precision. It is difficult, demanding labor. We cut a narrow trench, about two feet wide, in the moist red dirt. Then a second one goes on the other side of the crinum row. We slip steel shovels in at an angle, and rock and roll. We use the shovels to rock the massive clumps back and forth. We can hear the roots snap. Sooner or later, the hundred-pound weight of bulb, root, red dirt, and sleepy gray earthworms slumps onto its side, exposed. It's one huge clod! The individual bulbs don't want to be separated from their clump of friends. They hug each other tightly. But that's our work, to separate, sort by size, and replant for next summer's customers.

As soon as we get that clump to lean over, the physical work is almost over. Tom and I stand up and stretch. Maria and Ryan stay bent over their trench, still rocking. Two rows over, the donkey family—Daddy Buck, Justina, and Junior—hang out eating winter rye grass and remnants of sweet potatoes from the fall harvest. It's their winter treat to come into the lily field. They like the change in diet, and they like being right here with us.

Rows of bulbs wait their turn. At the edge of the field we see more flashes of bronze on a pink cloud tree, blue sky, and plowed khaki dirt in the background. Only one other thing

January
Sekki

13

moves—Sweetiepie, the dog, who's as busy as the bees. Sweetiepie, the hunter, doesn't succumb to the temptation to bask in the warm winter sun. Her nose is buried in the ground, tunneling for mouse or mole.

All this bulb-digging is actually all about inventory control and propagation. Inventory management for a crop of bulbs hidden in the earth is entirely different from managing bulbs grown in a container nursery. They're all underground here, and impossible to see or count. They huddle three feet below the layer of mulch and mice. When that clump is finally laid on its side, and backs and minds have paused awhile, we pull off the outer layer of baby bulbs—we call them pups—recreating that gentle, releasing, ripping sound again. It seems cruel, but we pry those pups off, still suckling at the mother bulb, with a knife or machete. We then start to sort the bulbs: mother size, teenagers, and baby size. All will go back in the ground in neat rows, organized by size. A layer of compost and a scattering of arugula seeds complete the job.

Along with the bees, we are all captivated for a moment by the tree full of winter flowers. Tom launches into a story about his mother's attempts to grow them. She wanted the fruit as well as the flowers. Satsuko, a war bride from Japan, moved across the globe to South Carolina with her soldier husband. Pregnant, like so many soldiers' wives, and with three little boys, she settled in a new climate with new plants and old memories. This plant that we call apricot, she knew as a salty pickled fruit snack called *umeboshi*. She wanted to grow a taste of home. Tom still makes little rice balls packed with *umeboshi* inside, a treat to remind him of his mom.

Tom's story about food reminds us that we're hungry. Momma rings the bell. She's laid out lunch on the kitchen table, something she always does no matter how many mouths she'll have to feed. A little blue jar of pink apricot flowers sits in the middle of the lunch table.

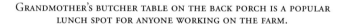

GRANDMOTHER'S BUTCHER TABLE ON THE BACK PORCH IS A POPULAR
LUNCH SPOT FOR ANYONE WORKING ON THE FARM.

Renovations

On any farm, people turn ideas, dirt, and endeavor into money by growing stuff other people want to buy. Crops change with cultural demands and decades. On this farm, earlier stewards of the land grew hay and cotton, but those farmers are long gone. Since at least the 1950s, all crops grown here have been associated with sustenance gardening for food unless we count the many crops of children raised here, too. But in 1990, we wanted the farm to begin to produce an income again. To be a farm again.

We had the good dirt, the muscle, and the enthusiasm, but we needed a new crop. We started thinking about our interests, about markets, and about our capacity. Getting into most new crops takes a lot of capital for new equipment and buildings. We didn't have that capital. Nor did we want to change the character of the well-worn

---

THE RENOVATED OLD CHICKEN HOUSE, WITH RAINBOW CORN-CRIB
SIDING, IS OUR NEW PACKING SHED.

---

place. We loved and valued the old rusty barns and the ancient pecan trees. We liked that wildflowers and weeds had taken over the pasture. We liked that the patched fence was more a memory of long-gone summer days packing posts with Daddy than it was a containment device for donkeys.

While we were scratching our heads, we realized that no matter the crop, the character of the place wasn't ours to change. Daddy had kept the roofs intact to protect our old buildings. These barns were my forts and playgrounds in the 1970s. I knew each of their secrets and every place where someone had carved their name. But once we decided on a new crop, the barns and buildings had to change in functional ways.

Today, with our new crop of lily bulbs and a more modern farm's new demands, like hosting visitors, we have to spend cold days on the continual stabilization, renovation, and repurposing of our barns. More than maintenance, January barn work includes engineering challenges like raising a roof to rebuild walls and creative challenges like making sure each old board tells its story—not just to me, but to the next generation of the family and to farm visitors.

Today the old chicken house is our shipping shed. Back in the 1930s, someone designed and built the perfect hen house—home to about 80 ladies. Once painted rusty red, the coop had been repaired with bits of yellow, white, green, and sky blue. For all of my life growing up here, it was rainbow-colored. Whoever built it was clever. He anticipated the needs of the working girls, but just as importantly, he laid it out for efficient poultry care and egg harvest. The structure was tall enough to walk through and had two separate rooms, one for poultry and another for prep and processing. Across from the screened wall, a gridded wall of nests had privacy and warmth. An easily accessible, eye-level hatch swung open for manure collection. This was at a time when manure was a valuable fertilizer. In fact, it was the only fertilizer. A fenced yard connected to the chicken house by a hickory-sapling gangplank thwarted predators. It functioned for fifty years and supported the feeding of a lot of people in those decades. In 1976, I made my first income from this farm, selling organic, free-range eggs from this chicken house. For seventy-five cents a dozen, I delivered anywhere up and down the dirt road, on a sparkly red-white-and-blue Sear's *Spirit of '76* bike.

We started lily farming in the field beyond the chicken house. The structure's location made it perfect for one of our new farm needs—cleaning, packing, and shipping lily bulbs. It was our first barn to undergo complete renovation. Even thinking of tearing it down hurt my heart. However, when the founder of the American School of Building Arts, John Paul Huguley, walked around the place, he gave me a bit of advice and therapy to get me through the change: "No one ever meant this building to last forever, Jenks. They built what they needed at the moment, with whatever scrap was lying around. They built it, patched it, and roofed it with boards left over from other projects. You love those layers. So photograph it, write about it, keep it, and keep the good boards, but tear it down and build something the farm needs now."

One frigid January morning, with Momma ruefully watching, we pulled that chicken house to the ground. My young nephew Robert hooked a chain between it and the truck. Tom pulled. It didn't take much. But then rather than condemning the old coop to the dump, we spent days separating out the rainbow-painted pine planks, the rusty tin, the hinges, and the grates. We would use all of them later to clad a new structure. This was an emotional day of changes. Besides the tear-down, it was also a commitment to a new crop, embarking into the unknown world of farming lilies. Today the little building looks a lot like it did fifty years ago. The new infrastructure and interior are designed for packing and shipping bulbs. But outside, it's a multi-colored chicken house, with slatted, corn-crib sides that let in a breeze. The same pine boards, rusty tin roof, and hinges all do what they've been doing for decades.

We did tart it up a bit. This "chicken house" has a 1970s acrylic chandelier complete with flashing, rainbow-colored lights. A hand-lettered sign salvaged from a local juke joint hangs on the front door, welcoming guests to Regina's Disco Lounge. But that's another story. The point here is that the old barn where I used to gather eggs is, in a way, the same barn from which we ship flower bulbs across the United States today.

Back in the 1970s, falling-down wooden buildings seemed to be everywhere. In overgrown fields or on edges of swamps, they had vines growing through them, treasure hidden inside, and sometimes an awful smelling wake of vultures living in the rafters. My buddies and I knew every abandoned barn for miles. We knew the treasures hidden inside. We knew their layouts and the likelihood of death by roof collapse or tongue-lashing by some old farmer.

We had two hideouts in different barn lofts. One of those lofts was tall enough that we could stand up at center, under the steel-gray tin and heart pine eaves. Walls and floors were built with gaps to let air flow, so even with doors closed we could observe everything going on outside. In the triangular end walls, one door looked over the backyard and the other over the farm and veggie garden. In the middle was a dangerous and exciting spot where someone had cut a few rafters to add a welding shed in the 1930s. We could stand side-by-side there, tempting fate by getting a little rhythm going and making the whole barn sway. Over the years, people had filled the loft with stuff: a ratty but plush purple Turkish carpet that belonged to my great grandmother, boxes of antique biology books, and old letters about running the farm. Here I had privacy with a view, a decent carpet, and science books. Heaven!

Our other loft hideout was not a real loft but an add-on in the top of a narrow, two-story smokehouse. We were lucky to have it. When these types of smokehouses went out of use, many got pulled down because the shape made them difficult to convert to something else. The lower part of ours became a cow barn. A rusted steel rung ladder ran straight up the wall to hooks at the top where things like meat or tobacco could be hung to dry. Someone added, way up there, a few planks to make a dark hideout complete with several *Playboy* magazines, probably from the 1950s. My buddies liked this place mostly for that reason. They'd get all worked up into some sort of group think— an attractive excitement in which they could have a communal conversation that I didn't really follow. While they huddled together, I'd be looking out the tiny window or looking back at them, always ready to go back to the loft with the better view and better books, where I didn't feel such separation.

There was a huge barn way out in the woods. It was gray cypress, riddled with worm tunnels, and with a loft the size of a tennis court. We thought this place was as remote and as lost as Atlantis. No one ever came out there. But Daddy said to beware because "hobos might sleep there." Totally empty, it was boring, but off to the side, was a little building with a tiny, sagging door. It was filled with treasure—boxes of sparkling rhinestones; jade-colored, tile-like jewelry with sphinxes carved into them; amber rings; and diamond-rope earrings. Even as a boy, I knew the difference between the masculine pieces of geometric design and the feminine pieces with beautiful sinuous, swooping lines. I liked both. I still love both, particularly in garden design with the contrast of refined details, fine gardening skills, and earthy craftsmanship. Elegance and Earth.

My buddies would put on jewelry and try to swish wrists and hips in that sad, Flip Wilson style of female impersonation. Their movements were too deep, arms bent into exaggerated waves and limp wrists, followed by lots of laughs. Maybe they were trying to look ridiculous out of fear. One of them, a redhead, always looked pretty good to me in jade. Maybe they knew what I was thinking, and they definitely knew that I could make the jewelry work for me—a bit too easily, too naturally for their comfort. We didn't play there a lot, not nearly as much as I wanted to. Besides, the purple-carpeted loft with its science books with illustrations on onion skin paper was my true haven anyway.

Today, on one corner of that barn, a climbing blue rose 'Veilchenbau' sends thick tendrils into the loft. Below it, a shrub rose 'Ruth's Tea Scented China' intertwines with head-high *Abelia chinesis*. Under that, periwinkle and spring snowdrops bloom. It's a simple planting that indicates the changes on the farm. In former days, flowers would have gotten in the way of work. Now they make the barn seem romantic and rooted. The funny thing is, when I once asked an old man who grew up playing here about the barn's main functions back in the 1950s, he said, "I don't remember that barn ever being used for work! But we sure played all over and in it!"

We spent a cold week one January jacking up and stabilizing that barn's roof. This required cutting holes in the floors of the barn and its loft. Then we slid in old 6 x 6

THE OLD WOODSHED, WITH COB WALLS, NOW ACTS AS A
GUEST SPACE AND SMALL CLASSROOM.

posts vertically and balanced them on hydraulic jacks. Finally, we pumped in unison
on the jacks and slowly lifted the entire roof—suspending for a moment thousands of
pounds of heart pine, tin, and memories. It was creaky, scary, and kind of magical. Like
the boys who used to sway here in the loft, we found the barn's limits again. When the
barn was stabilized, we built in a new support structure and let the old roof back down
onto the renewed barn.

From the outside, the original 1890s barn looks the same—wide heart pine planks,
soaked in decades of barn-red stain, and streaked with yellow algae. On the inside, the
barn is part of the farm's new cycle. Today, it holds tools specific to our lily farming
and even a small classroom, where we share lessons from our new endeavor. The barn
represents where we came from and where we are going.

A FIELD OF TOADFLAX TELLS EVERYONE SPRING IS
JUST AROUND THE CORNER.

Toadflax Haze

The promise pops up throughout the rural south in mid-February. Fallow farm fields transform into endless embroidered meadows of lavender, burgundy, and gold. These fields of toadflax, wild mustard, and sour grass tell me the earth has shifted back toward the sun, and the ground is warming although the air is still cold. Toadflax promises spring will come soon.

I drive a lot in winter. I'm on the road to do presentations and book signings and to help gardeners and farmers plan their land. I get to see the fields change. In January the fields look like a blond five-o'clock shadow with their faded stubble of corn stalks. Soon there will be a little fuzzy coating of green. The sequence is the same, even in different parts of the state. In the Sandhills' white sands, the Pee Dee's black muck, and the Low Country's gray fields, the same pattern of change unfolds. The distant background changes, too, from rolling hills with silos to tobacco barns, to a herd of fat cows, even newly sprouted subdivisions. No matter the picture or the soil color, farm fields in February all get coated with a low and fine winter-growing green mat.

Get out and look closely. You'll see that the green mat is actually a community of different seedlings. Scalloped leaves from afar become purple henbit close up. Spoon-shaped, elongated thick leaves reveal burgundy sour grass. Wide, round, grayish seedlings are actually yellow wild mustard. All these plants are from Europe and are soon to be part of a tapestry in the lavender mist of American toadflax *(Nuttallanthus canadensis)*.

In the mixed community of green, the tiniest and frailest plants are the toadflax. Their delicate, thread-like leaves emerge from a central point. If you pull one, you get a white tap root, no bigger than a toothpick, with a flat cap of green threads radiating outward. Fragile as they seem, they're tough enough to grow with the other weeds and will soon produce the dominant lavender color displayed in the multi-colored fields.

In early February, by leaps and bounds, the mustards become foot-wide clumps, with sparse golden flowers for the bees. A few weeks later, a furry carpet of rounded apple-green leaves and a dusting of deep purple henbit flowers covers the ground. All pretty, but only a precursor to the moment of toadflax and sour grass.

The burgundy is sour grass. Children chew the stalks to make their mouths water. Old farmers say sour grass means the soil needs lime. It's not a true grass, but single stalks rise to about a foot tall, topped with a thick beard of tiny burgundy flowers *(Rumex acetosella)*.

The floating lavender haze seems to weave all together like magic, hiding the fragile stems that hold up the flowers. When you notice the lavender haze in the distance, you might want to run through it, to lay claim to it. But if you do, you'll see that the lavender magic is always just a few feet ahead. It's kind of trippy to be in the toadflax mist. It's like chasing a cloud. Look across the field at this overwhelming display, and you can see right through to the ground. Kneel and look more closely. Each flower is the size of the head of a pin and needs a magnifying glass to reveal its labia, the glowing blonde hairs inside. You can get lost in the intricate design of the tiny flowers just as easily as you can get lost contemplating the big picture of those clouds of toadflax hovering in the meadow.

I know it's only pick-up truck philosophizing, but happiness in life is kind of like a field of toadflax. Happiness will be just ahead, right? Finding the perfect job, person, or hobby is just like trying to find and sit on that beautiful carpet of toadflax. It's always a little further on. It's about perspective. It's all about how you choose to look out and see the world. Get happy right where you're standing.

If you're lucky, when you stand on the side of some country road, admiring this flowering phenomenon growing in a field, it will be part of some quaint scene. Perhaps an old silo, a rusty fence, a herd of fat beef cows on the other side of the field looking back at you. But what if they're not looking at you at all? What if they're lost in thought, admiring the lavender mist just like you are? Maybe they take you in only as a part of the scene, some distant background for the majesty of the tapestry of color between them and you. Wait. Stop the music and clear the haze. More likely, those heifers are just wondering if you might be about to open a gate so they can come in to munch down on that lavender mist.

THE BURGUNDY OF SOUR GRASS STARTS EARLY AND LASTS THROUGH
THE MONTH, EVEN AS TOADFLAX STARTS TO FADE.

The Smells of Smoke

Farming used to be more communal. Neighbors helped each other build barns, clear fields, and do work that came in big batches. Around here, where people grew hay, we'd help each other out when the baled hay was still in the field and a big thunderstorm was coming in. Mechanization has reduced dependence on friends. One person with a tractor and a specialized loader can stack a load of hay, a task that used to take three people. By the 1970s, most farmers in these parts also had to have off-farm jobs. With more commitments and more individual power derived from efficient equipment, communal work days went by the wayside. But even then, local farmers and their sons still got together for one of the last remaining communal work projects—managing controlled burns. Today the smell of smoke can take me back to those not-so-long-ago times when burning hayfields brought men and boys together.

WE BREAK OUT OUR HEAVY BOOTS WHEN WE BURN OUR
FIELDS TO CONTROL WOODY WEEDS.

I remember those cold Saturday mornings. On one farm after another, small crews of experienced, trusted men started the work early. They prepped for the burn day by creating safety zones and fire breaks to manage the very controlled fires around the barns or woodlines.

As the day warmed up, all my friends and their brothers showed up on our farm. They arrived in their beaters, those old banged-up trucks perfect for farm work. Some beaters weren't even roadworthy, with their hoods tied down with baling twine or such, but most were a little better than Daddy's old truck. It was a Dodge. Salvaged from the US Forestry Service, it had all sorts of official lettering and logos on its side. At some point, someone had tried to cover them with squiggles of army green spray paint. The old truck had holes rusted right through the floorboards. No one had ever done anything about them, but that didn't matter. It was built like a tank. There was even a cavernous space under the hood with two shelves for tools or a toolbox.

One cold morning riding in the truck, we heard a soft purr everytime we came to a stop. Daddy supposed a leaking hose was making the noise. Eventually it turned into a full-blown meow. When we pulled over under a magnolia tree, we opened the hood and found a kitten riding around on the tool shelf. Most men would have sent that kitty away, but Daddy wanted to keep her warm inside the truck. She ended up staying on the farm about as long as that old truck. She grew to love burn days because the flames chased rodents from their winter nests.

By mid morning on the burn day, we boys would have our flat shovels in hand and walk ahead of the flame line. Our job was to watch for rouge flames leaping out ahead of the line. We would slap them down with the shovels or stomp them out with our boots. My brogans, saturated with neatsfoot oil, absorbed the smell of smoke and the ash from the fires, so they left black smudges everywhere I wore them all winter.

Generally the fire was never more than knee high. It all seemed orderly and predictable. The low flames gave off hay-scented smoke. I don't recall ever worrying about the fire getting out of control, but I know that the experienced crew kept alert for any danger to barns, trucks, tractors, woods, or boys—probably in that order.

During the same decade, but in the more suburban setting of Dentsville, South Carolina, close to Fort Jackson army base, Tom's dad also burned his land, except his land was a lawn. Like ours, their lawn-burning day was a day for men and boys. These guys were used to working together. They were soldiers from all over the country pulled together by duty or retirement. The GI bill helped them get housing loans and led to the development of unique suburbs of families all about the same age. Many of these guys settled into new track houses with wives they'd brought with them from all over the world.

Tom's dad, a first-generation Irish American, served in Japan just after the occupation. He met and married Satsuko there. She was a stunning young woman who'd been a model. They moved their international family to one of these suburbs, teaming with children. They settled into their neighborhood with its mix of families that included Germans, Puerto Ricans, and Koreans. In many ways, the families in these suburbs defined modern America.

Satsuko wanted her children to be all-American. She didn't teach them to speak Japanese or explore their Japanese heritage. She wanted Tom to do American-boy things, like burning the grass with the men. But in her yard, traces of home grew—a Japanese Apricot tree and a tightly sheared cloud bush. Next door, the German-American family's yard had colorful flower boxes. Down the road, the Latin-American family had a giant agave plant. It was a diverse and strong community. The families in that neighborhood, much like the farm families I grew up around, understood the importance of staying connected and coming together for each other. They understood that simple events like lawn-burning days had a deeper purpose, something beyond the utilitarian.

Endless lawns in brand new suburbs aren't all that different from a pasture of hay when it comes to managing a controlled burn. Lots of these men had once been farm boys. They knew how to burn. Once a year the men borrowed drip torches from the fort's forestry crews, and just like on our farm, men and boys made a day of managing fires of the controlled burns.

Unfortunately, burn days for us are no longer communal. Technology lets Tom and me do this alone. Extensive underground piping gives us access to water to saturate certain areas for preventative protection and, if needed, for control. From the field, in real time, we can check in with the Forestry Service, which approves or rejects our burn permits based on detailed weather data.

Professional foresters across the US still use prescribed burns to reduce the chance and intensity of wildfires. Keeping dry brush accumulation low means less fuel for future fires. It minimizes carbon release and potential devastation to homes. Fires also control pests. Foresters know which trees can tolerate a burn and at which point in their growing cycle to perform the burn. The result is that the flames kill certain plants while encouraging the growth of others.

Today on our farm, we burn our lily fields to kill perennial and woody weeds. Remember that the lily bulb crop on the farm takes three to four years to mature. That means we contend with perennial and woody weeds such as native cherry laurel and Virginia creeper. We have only two ways to deal with those weeds—pull or burn. If we burn, we get the added benefit of being able to control spittlebugs, ticks, and grasshoppers that burrow down in the dry grass for protection from the cold. Burning is effective and efficient. Plus respectfully using the power of fire as a tool is a connection to the past. It feels primal, and I look forward to it on cold days.

Ash from the burns quickly adds potassium and phosphorus to the soil. These nutrients are essential for plant growth. Some other elements in the soil are chemically bound, not usable by plants if the soil pH is too low, as ours usually is. Ash has a high pH. In farmer language, ash sweetens the soil. Sweet and warm. What more can you want on a cold February day?

There's another way that burning helps build soil fertility. After the thatch is burned away, the sun warms the ground, encouraging early growth. Seeds of cover crops, like clover and vetch, germinate uniformly. Later as the clover turns into thatch, it releases nitrogen for our lilies.

Besides prescribed burns on the fields, we have another type of winter burn that is equally important—brush pile fires. During the year, we pile up debris in the middle of a pasture. The debris is from storm cleanup and windrow pruning and fence repair. These brush piles get bigger and bigger all season, and fire turns them into useful ashes.

My heart breaks a little on brush pile burn days. Wildlife needs a pile. Bluebirds use it as a quick place to hide from hawks. Quail, like the bobwhite, and other ground-nesting birds gain protection from the piled limbs. Rabbits, rats, toads, and snakes use the pile as a condo. Before I start a brush pile fire, I always speak to the animals. I warn them to head out, to seek a new home. Then I'm careful never to burn the pile completely nor too quickly.

Everyone, especially Momma, loves a winter burn. On days when Momma's reluctant to leave the house, I can entice her with the promise of a brush-pile fire. She knows she needs winter exercise, and for the success of the fire, she knows how to feed it properly. She loves the noises of Carolina cherry laurels as they snap, crackle, and pop. The bamboo canes make the best noises though. Without question bamboo's name comes from the sound of gunshots the canes make when they burn—bam, bam, boom! It frightens dogs and delights children. Wait—who am I kidding? It delights Momma and me, too.

Every fire brings back memories. It's something about the fragrances in the smoke. Tonight I can smell the fragrance of incense cedar logs as the smoke billows up through fresh green boughs. It's powerful magic, conjuring up memories that tumble around inside my head: an old Berol pencil sharpener, the shavings spilling out; a windy winter day; primeval fairytale forests. I think of climbing through canopies, warming myself by the woodstove, working in a burning hayfield, pausing to watch the smoke and flames and friends and fathers, and somehow sensing that I'm witnessing a future memory coming together.

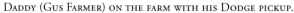

DADDY (GUS FARMER) ON THE FARM WITH HIS DODGE PICKUP.

The Bulb Lawn

March makes me laugh at the carnival of colors. It's totally gaudy, like the fair at night. It's the exact opposite of what color wheels say are tasteful combinations, and it blows in the face of garden designers' artifice of color-themed, color-echoing, perennial borders. We live the whole of March in swirlings of rowdy color.

Curtains of purple wisteria dotted with yellow Carolina jessamine cascade from the trees. The massive vines climb for light, wrapping trunks, then crawling across the canopy. You can see the extent of coverage only from high above it, from the highest peak of the roof, but you can sense it by smell from the ground. Wisteria's purple fragrance makes for a special spring moment.

Everyone who comes to visit in late March stops to admire one spot closer to the ground—the bulb lawn. A carpet of tiny flowers covers the entire side yard of the house.

COMMONLY CALLED GRAPE HYACINTH, OLD SOUTHERN GARDENERS CALL
THIS BABY'S BREATH FOR ITS CLOYING FRAGRANCE.

It's romantically beautiful for a moment. At first glance, it seems to be an endless quilt of white lacy stars of Bethlehem. In reality, many species and colors of tiny bulbs are in the mix—all planted or naturalized since 1905. They've found their favorite spots in the lawn. Some like the hot, dry spot by the dusty road, and some like the moisture and shade near the house. Others prefer the middle ground. Flowering together in March, all the little bulbs signal the coming of summer and the end of early spring.

The dominant bulbs are stars of Bethlehem. Each five-inch-tall stem holds a dozen star-shaped flowers. Though real stars come out at night, these little flowers close at night and on cloudy days. So a bright sunny day is the best time to see the bulb lawn. Stars cover it like a dusting of snow.

Stars of Bethlehem scatter their seeds, so new plants pop up anywhere and everywhere. Walking around southern woodlands today, you'll see stars of Bethlehem mixed into the wildflowers. They're a widespread species, thriving in Africa, Asia, Europe, and now in our own woodlands. One of the important take-aways from understanding the journey of flora like the star of Bethlehem is that the mix of spring flowers in the wild changes over time. That mix was changing long before people were around. Plants moved with continental drift, birds, ice flows, and storms. We can look back at a moment in time and get a snapshot of what our "virgin" woodlands were like. That picture, however, is just a single moment—a nostalgic image frozen in time. It is as romanticised as the picture of the bulb lawn that I've painted for you in this essay. Glorious for a few weeks in March, in my memory, but quickly changing to something else soon enough. Fifty million years ago star of Bethlehem and wisteria may not have been here. Now they are part of our southern flora. Ecosystems modify, accept, exchange, and hybridize themselves. We are part of that change, too, and we need to be stewards of the ecosystem, not dictators of it.

In the lily fields, it's a different matter entirely. A farm is intentionally a semi-monoculture. Customers count on getting crinums from us, free of stowaways—extra plants of any kind—no matter how charming. We work to keep the fields free of unwanted plants that might get caught up in the crinums' roots and hitch a ride to a customer's garden. Star of Bethlehem is easy to keep at bay in this artificially, intentionally pure farm field. We simply mow them down to keep them from flowering and setting seed near the fields.

As big and bold as the bulb lawn is, my favorite tiny bulb requires you to get down on hands and knees to really enjoy it. Baby's breath, *Muscari neglectum,* flowers deep plum purple with a hint of steel gray. Its lentil-sized individual flowers are stacked like beads on a tiny Christmas tree. The topmost flowers shine baby blue. But the main attraction is invisible, a sweetness that some find cloying like honey and almond. Intense as it is, it's a fragrance you have to stoop to catch. It doesn't flow through the air at people height. It must float somehow though, because hairy-footed bees and lots of different types of flies are drawn to it. They pollinate these tiny flowers, which then set seeds. Here in our yard, the true species of *Muscari neglectum* spreads itself around. You can buy similar plants from a commercial bulb supplier today. It's sold as grape hyacinth. They're beautiful plants, but I've never seen the modern versions set seeds or naturalize. Muscari like the hottest, driest parts of the yard out by the dusty road where a red cedar and thick zoysia suck up all the summer moisture.

At the other end of the yard, where things are a little shady and moist, pink oxalis thrives. These are not true bulbs but tubers. Oxalis is called wood sorrel, but you may also hear it called shamrocks or clover. Some people mistake it for a weed. I can see why people think that, since it makes little green humps in the grass. To people who like a perfect, crew-cut lawn, it messes up the picture. Y'all just relax. Forget the perfect lawn and stop and smell the sorrel. As March turns to April, a little more heat will be in the air, and those leaves and flowers will wither. Below ground, tiny tubers remain through the summer. They'll follow the same routine for decades, surfacing next spring to see who's still around and who's new on the farm. Those tubers look like tiny white potatoes, and they've been used all over the world for food. The leaves and flowers, like sour grass, have a refreshing sweet-and-sour taste because they contain oxalate crystals, which make your mouth water.

Somewhere in between the muscari and the oxalis, in the middle of the yard, a few special tulips pop up—ones we've planted over the past decades. Most tulips do not persist well in our climate, but a few actually spread themselves around. *Tulipa chrysantha* is called lady tulip or peppermint tulip. It has pencil-sized gray leaves and thumb-sized yellow flowers that open and close with the sun. My niece Caroline and I once planted a few hundred of these in the outline of a heart. It was a sweet idea, a springtime suprise for Momma. Although the planting never made the dramatic display we envisioned, we still hunt for it each year, check on it, take a picture, and remember that day of working together and dreaming of our big yellow tulip heart.

A bulb lawn and a tidy lawn simply do not go together. After flowering, in the last week of March, it takes lots of restraint not to cut the messy-looking foliage. Let the bulb leaves wither. Bulbs need the leaves to make energy for next year. By May, you start mowing, the grass greens up, and the lawn looks normal. By fall, little green bulb leaves peak through just after the grass turns brown. In mid-February, we give it a cut with a mower raised high. This high haircut lets the coming flowers show more clearly when they explode in March.

Spring bulbs pushing through the grass bring to my mind the doyen of the Beech Island Garden Club, Miss Bertha Atkinson. She had a beautifully layered yard filled with plant treasures. As part of my job on Atkinson farms, I was often assigned to Miss Bertha as garden helper for spring cleanup days. One warm March day in the early '80s still comes to mind this time of year. It was the day when she offered me an animated lesson in bulb care and gender roles. I had started mowing her lawn, which was messy and ragged with jonquil and star of Bethlehem leaves. In the moment I was proud of myself for having been so proactive. Miss Bertha, I soon discovered, was not. She hurried over to me, frustrated and making vigorous and repeated hand signals to stop. You know the one—slicing fingers across the neck. When she finally got me to shut off the mower, Miss Bertha intoned, "Remember all those flowers a few weeks ago? The jonquils and stars of Bethlehem! For them to do that next year, they need their leaves to stay green. You can't mow them now." Then she looked me square in the eye and ended with, "Men always want to mow too early. Why don't they understand mowing will kill the jonquils?"

As March wanes, I watch the flowers fade and the bulb lawn grow ragged. I want to mow, to tidy up the picture. But I stop to listen to what Mrs. Bertha would surely tell me, in her stern voice, now warmed by time and nostalgia, "Don't be one of *those* men Jenks. Be a caretaker. Embrace the change. Save the jonquils."

Stars of Bethlehem blanket the bulb lawn, and
Lady Banks rose flowers by the woodshed.

$\mathcal{E}$*arthen Warmth*

It's an optimistic time—or presumptive. March means planning and planting the seeds that will become flowery moments, supper, and summer plant sales.

Starting seeds this time of year takes vision. The lily fields look terrible. Since the ground is warming, all the bulbs' pent-up energy starts to flow. Force pushes leaves out from deep underground faster than the foliage can change from white to green. Like raw turkey parts, slightly vulgar protrusions of necks bulge up through fire-blackened hay— big necks, little necks, necks that get caught and bent, extruded, and etiolated. Sometimes new leaves can't unfurl, they get bound together with last year's dried up leaves. Like watching a birth, seeing crinum emerge in March is powerful, but not pretty.

A miniature meadow of new ryegrass is coming up among all this. Milky jade-green, youthful peach fuzz glistens with dew in morning light and softens the blackened field.

EARLY SPRING BED PREPARATION STARTS WITH CHOPPING WINTER COVER
CROPS LIKE RYEGRASS, THEN LAYERING FIELDS WITH BERMUDA HAY.

We didn't plant the winter rye. We don't even like it. But it comes every year, and given the seed bank in the surrounding fields, rye will be here longer than we will. We search for its virtue. One good thing rye does is make a massive root system that tills the soil. That process pulls nutrients from deep down in the red clay. Later the same roots, as they decay, act as a down elevator for microorganisms and insects.

Through earthen magic and warmth, those little rye seedlings jump to eighteen inches and make a handsome companion to the early crinum flowers. But soon enough, the growth becomes an overwhelming wolfman's beard. We have to manage it or it will shade out seedlings, poppies, cabbage, and lilies. So we find a balance. That means we kill some of it with a mist of vinegar from a backpack sprayer. Not a kitchen vinegar, it's extra strong. Applied now, vinegar kills tender weeds, but it doesn't bother perennials, including lily bulbs.

After the vinegar spray, shriveled rye and mulch get raked off to expose the soil. Red sandy stripes raked clean through blackened mulch let warming sunlight hit the earth. New seedlings of nasturtium and beans jump up. We seed in two ways. The first is simply poking a hole in the dirt with a stick and dropping in a seed. Sometimes, we use a walk-behind Earthway seeder, as it gives very straight rows and even spacing. Either way, big hopes go in those holes.

When is optimistic different from presumptive? Is it all going to live and feed us and make pretty pictures for farm visitors? I'm optimistic. Will those visitors come at all? Will I even see or taste what I'm planting or will my turn to be planted in a hole come first? I'm presumptive.

I might as well enjoy my hands in the dirt today. I like my hands when they're coated with red crust, cradling and sorting seeds. My back needs a rest though, so I stand up and look around at still more work to be done. A bent fence needs repair. Might as well imagine it blanketed with cucumber vines. The raw opening in the pasture of that freshly dug trench is like a red wound revealing a few bones of broken irrigation tubing near the gate. Let it all be healed and woven with Bermuda grass. There's the little donkey, Buck Jr., looking like a toy. He needs to be lured into a corral, wrestled into a trailer, and delivered to his new owner. No need to worry about that daunting task or the broken jaw that may come with it. I just picture him being king in his new domain. He's going on to another farm, where they need a donkey to love their goats, to play with them, and to protect them from coyotes. All that other farm work has to wait for another day, so I squat back down. This March day has to be for seeds. March seeding is really dreaming of the sekki moments of summer.

For some seedlings, it's been quite a journey. They're already up as tiny rosettes of green lying flat on the ground. I remember that misty night back in October when I put on a big hat with lights, strapped a seed spreader onto my chest, scaring the donkeys, and whirled out pounds of seed. That was the start of a powerful process. The mist and seeds soon made roots no bigger than arm hairs. They found a home. Through the flood of winter rain, the ice sheet in January, grazing donkeys and fire over the fields in February, those winter-growing seedlings anchored down. Now with sun energy beaming down on them, they need a little extra care to launch. Some appreciate a mist of liquid fish emulsion. Plants, like people need fatty acids. Some appreciate the sunshine we let in by burning and killing rye grass with vinegar. Some need mowing. Purple henbit was just a downy coat of green yesterday, but today is shading everything else. A quick cut over the top lets the larkspur seedlings see the sun again.

Some seedlings need watching over. Quarter-size spinach plants and the new shoots of potatoes can get cold damage this time of year. The earth, warming as the rays of sun become more direct, contains more heat. The seedlings want to grow, but there's still danger from the clear night sky. It surrounds them with clouds of chilly air. We cover those tiny plants with mulch. Our job is not to cover up the tiny plants to protect them from the descending chill, but to let the mulch capture the heat of the earth that's being released while the sun is gone. The mulch creates a little warm layer over the ground, around the spinach and the new shoots of potatoes. It's insulation. The temperature tells us which kind of mulch to use. Just like some sweater fabrics capture the heat of your body better than others, some types of mulch capture the heat of the earth better than others. For the spinach and potatoes or anything else tender, an open layer of straw over the top is like a cotton sweater. If an arctic cold blast is coming, we need to use a thicker and denser layer of mulch, like a wool sweater. Sometimes we'll even use a frost blanket to insulate the few inches of air just above the ground, protecting the spinach and new potato shoots by catching the heat released from the ground.

Another kind of work happens inside in March before the suns comes up and before hands get dirty. The work that's harder and more unpleasant for me is figuring out how to get garden clubs, master gardeners, and other guests to sign up for summer tours. I text, I Facebook, and I coordinate lunches and buses and brochure descriptions. Presumption looms in my little office as I think about their visits to the farm after learning that we're here. Then here are these brilliantly colorful, sunny days of March. Optimism infuses them as dreams start to become real with the springing-up of all those seedlings and the coming together of new friends on the farm.

Lily Lust

The first crinum to flower marks the start of the spectacular lily season. Wide gray leaves squeeze up like tongues coming out of the earth. Then from between the pressed-together leaves a tip, a veiled green spear, peeks out. That's the bud. It's a masculine phallic thing. Nonetheless, I always think of this first crinum as feminine, maybe because that first flowering seems like a long-awaited birth. Or maybe it's because the awesome life force emerges from deep under the earth. It starts slowly. Then one morning, shimmery wet green buds burst open, and rich blood-pink and white lilies seem to float across the foggy field.

It's a moment that stops me in my tracks.

Crinum bulbispermum is called Orange River lily, for the longest river in South Africa, her homeland. Around here it's called cemetery lily since it was traditionally planted on graves and still comes up in old cemeteries. You'll find her on roadsides too, among the remnant plants marking empty places that used to be busy, fertile homes and gardens. She's rooted into the South, renewing herself, rebirthing each spring.

I was ten when I met my first lovely Orange River lily. She was fifty years old. I fell in love. Her flowers drew me to her. And something about the way those gray leaves unfurled to reveal a soft secret. They emerged rolled-up but flattened out to be wider than my hand. Though they look tough, the leaves are tender. But what gets every young man who falls in love with a lily is the mystery, the intrigue of what might be hidden deep below in the earth, the divine feminine.

I didn't treat her so well, my first Orange River lily. All of my buddies liked the leaves, though they weren't drawn to plants. They thought that the waist-high mound of leaves, surrounded by a flat zoysia lawn, was the perfect spot to make a bike obstacle course, and she was the perfect obstacle. And I had the tools and skills to make it happen. One thing Daddy gave me that helped me fit in with the other boys was a good tool box and great building skills. We—mainly me—built a little wooden ramp. From the edge of the grass and with a long speed build-up, we'd go up the ramp and right over my lily if we were successful. More often, for the younger fellas like me, we'd crash straight into her. Towheaded Mike, the tallest and oldest among us, already with golden fleece on his long legs, could do it best. He could jump the lily without touching a leaf. Then he'd wait for our admiration and for one of us to crash.

I'd rather have been picking flowers or digging in the red clay to see how far down my

---

For its pastel greens and various shades of pink, our selection of
Orange River lily is called 'Aurora Glorialis'.

lady lived. The fellas would go home, leaving gray leaves scattered across the lawn, unimpressed that no other crinum has leaves that color. I'd take care of her, clean her up, prune her to the raw white inner leaves jutting straight up from the ground. She looked exposed and damaged after our time with her. But she'd be OK. This very same bulb is ninety years old now. My first love thrives and flowers with yellow Japanese kerria and running lavender phlox at her feet.

Orange River lily flowers the second week in April here in Zone 8b. But planted against a warming wall, flowers erupt earlier. Andy Cabe, Curator of nearby Riverbanks Botanical Garden, says he's seen *Crinum bulbispermum* bloom as early as December or January. In places with warmer climates like New Orleans or Orlando, blooms come a lot sooner. In colder places like Saint Louis or Connecticut, flowers peak in mid to late May. Lee Buttala in Bridgewater, Connecticut, says, "When I first planted *Crinum bulbispermum* in my Zone 5/6 garden, I had little hope of it overwintering one season, let alone four. Since then, there has been nothing more satisfying than its flowers in mid-May. I tell other Zone 5 gardeners how I just cut back its foliage and leave it alone over winter. They aren't too sure about that answer. Then they smile when I pass along one of its giant seeds."

The common name suggests that Orange River lily may flower orange or at least be a good water plant. Neither is true. In southern Africa, rains come, bringing floods, followed by months of drought. She needs the cycle. Drought, dormancy, followed by a long period of growth which includes flowering and fruiting. Our winter induces the same long dormancy. This tolerance to extremes makes *Crinum bulbispermum* a perfect plant for rain gardens, drainage swales, and even green roofs.

As summer heat arrives, flower stalks fall over, laden with veiny green sacks of seeds. These seeds have an amazing adaptation: they photosynthesize. Typical seeds, say a bean or a nut, are dry brown storage packets. But these fleshy green seeds are almost like leaves, collecting solar energy and storing water to feed the growing seedling. A worm-like white tap root curves out of the seed, down deep into the womb of the earth, where a new tiny bulb forms. New leaves emerge down there, too, protected from drying weather and from grazing wildlife. When those leaves finally come up for air and light, the green seed fades away, having nursed the seedling through the first few months of life.

Growing crinums from seed is kind of addictive. Dive into this process yourself. Collect seeds and sow them in a pot. The simple act of picking these amazing seeds is rewarding. Each is different, and you won't want to miss one. I started collecting them from my first Orange River back in the '70s and still do it every year. I've grown tens of thousands. It takes three or four years to go from seed to flower. As with any sexual propagation, the babies range from big to little, spectacular to dull, white to rich pink, and everything in between. Like children or puppies, most grow up to be just fine.

But some turn out to be spectacular. Around 2004, I noticed a standout in the field of flowers. I've worked with her, learning to propagate, to duplicate, learning when flowers emerge and how tall they grow, getting ready to share with friends, and to sell. After evaluations from Missouri Botanical Garden in St. Louis as well as from friends in Orlando and Washington DC, I know she's an amazing garden plant. On day one, she blooms her new flowers' green petals. On the second day, those fade to pale pink, and new green buds opened. The third day sees the pale pink petals change to rich rose. She puts on a real show.

Since I originated, selected, and prepared this new plant, I got to name her. With all three soft colors bursting in her flowers, *aurora borealis* came to mind. But to honor Momma, Gloria Farmer, who raised me on the farm, who encouraged me to dig and explore my first crinum love, this stunning garden plant became 'Aurora Glorialis'.

They are the ladies I love, equally elegant, feminine, and grounded in our red dirt.

COLLECTING THE FAT, FLESHY SEEDS OF ORANGE RIVER LILY CAN BE ADDICTIVE. THE SEEDS TAKE THREE OR FOUR YEARS TO GROW TO FLOWERING-SIZE BULBS.

Dripping Honey

At our farm the transition to a new crop began slowly. Sales were sluggish. We thought that growing something lovely meant people would buy.

Did I really expect cars simply to roll down the muddy country road and customers to show up for a box of massive brown bulbs that look like pithy onions? Well, kind of. The bulbs may take awhile to show their colors, but just look at those flowers, those sculptural leaves, those grand bulbs. They're stunning!

But what do I know? When I was a naive college freshman. I put an application in for a killer job at a renowned botanical garden in England, thinking I was hot shit. I was sure they'd hire me right off the bat. According to their try-again-next-year letter, they needed some convincing and I needed some experience.

THE BEES IN THE HIVES AND THE WILD BEES THAT LIVE IN THE WALLS AND CEILINGS OF THE HOUSE HAVE BEEN THRIVING SINCE THE TRANSITION TO ORGANIC FARMING.

In this new venture, we needed to have more marketing experience under our belts to attract people new to crinum lilies. We brainstormed and then in April, when huge candy-stripe flowers popped up, we took pictures. We wrote stories. We started going to garden shows, sending photos to magazines, offering special Lily Field Days and Farm Open Days, complete with a glass of crinum tea and a piece of Momma's pound cake for every guest.

As it turned out, despite our lack of marketing experience, we were able to survive the transition. Simultaneously, we embarked on another one. And this transition would also end up transforming our marketing efforts, making us educators more than marketers.

Throughout my career, I have tried to encourage people to go organic. I may have inspired a few but I've also tried to push a donkey into a trailer. The first step seems impossible. In the end, I found it better to lead by example. So in the lily fields, we made the huge transition back to organic gardening. People had done it on this land before. Like the indigenous people and early settlers who had no choice. Like a few of the early plantation planters. In the 1940s came decades of conventional farming and synthetic fertilizer. But in the 1970s, Daddy started a transition to no-till soil building. We built on what he had started—testing, mixing old ideas with new technology, searching for ways to coax the best from the land without harming it. With this sort of experimentation, we came up with new fertility systems and work routines. We also needed new helpers and a new type of worker who got it and wanted to help explain it all to visitors. Going organic became part of our marketing. Compromises and attitude adjustments came, too. Results and rewards slowly followed. None was so unexpected as the population explosion of pollinating insects. Springtime brought lilies and our usual honey bees but also beautiful species of butterflies, moths, wasps, spiders and metallic jade-green flies that we'd never seen before.

When we moved into this 1750s farmhouse in the early 1970s, plaster fell from the ceilings. Porches sagged, and people would look up at the front corner of the house and say "How you gonna get those bees out of there? They'll ruin the house. They'll get into the bedrooms and sting you at night." or "Wonder what they do to make that big black stain on the siding and window trim."

Daddy crafted his own solution. He figured those bees were here before we were, and they'd stay. One Saturday night after supper, he was working in the wood shop with machines buzzing, making some mysterious contraption. Early the next morning, while the bees were still huddled in the honeycomb, we leaned a forty-foot ladder against the house and screwed a series of wooden blocks over their entry hole. We painted quickly. He'd made them a landing pad with tunnels through the blocks. To this day, they still use the pad to come and go, to do their little bee dances, leaving their dirty footprints atop the platform, out of our sight. Window trim and woodwork stay clean. There's still nothing to do about the brown spot in the parlor ceiling. No stain-blocking paint works on a constant drip of fresh honey that is inaccessible to harvest. We take friends into the bedroom to press an ear against the plaster walls to hear the hum. It is what it is.

We feel a duty to manage the balance of life. We need the pollinators and all the little connectors of life even when we don't understand them all. Good farmers, nurturing farmers, try to understand, try to share the farm with the life that's there.

Daddy started that important soil transition that we build on today. He took land back from decades of over-tilled, conventional farming. He paid a small price by giving up rent from a soybean farmer to convert the over-tilled land from soybeans to perennial bermuda hay. Like so many post-depression children, he'd seen the southern soil catastrophe left by careless cotton farmers. Almost all land in the South was devastated, left eroded down to hard red clay. Most of the South was denuded land that could no long grow food. Hunger, malnutrition, and poverty ensued. If you ever read *Tobacco Road,* you have a sense of the hard reality of those difficult times—truth in fiction. Luckily, people of Daddy's generation saw government programs repair damaged land. They learned practices like contour farming, cover cropping, windrowing, and planting pine and kudzu—all conservation practices that hold abused, eroding soil in place. This began the process of building soil. Daddy had vision. He knew a balance between farming, managing the land, and encouraging life could be achieved.

There are real costs to these sorts of transitions. Honey dripping in the living room is a real cost. More manual labor is a real cost. For the lilies, no-till soil building and other organic management practices mean a slower production time, more rodents, more pests, and higher labor costs. Organic farming means we have weeds. And it means we get to explain to people what we're doing and why it's important to us, to them, and to the health of our bugs and our society. We tell people our farm is organically managed. In most ways, we go far beyond the typical definition of organic farming, but we do make a concession, as we use seasonal ant killer on our grassy walkways. I could give you all my justifications, but mostly, it is part of our marketing strategy. Garden club ladies don't like fire ants biting them.

Roger Swain, the host of America's long-running public TV show, *Victory Garden,* helped me figure out what to call what we do. Technically and legally, we can't call ourselves an organic farm. Roger, a sardonic New Englander, said we need an acronym that sounds professional and complicated. So we call it PMO—Pretty Much Organic.

The fertility system we came up with is what we call Sheet Composting. We could call it SCSCSC, since it involves layers. It's not too different from the methods in that amazing little book, *Lasagna Gardening.* It means we layer organic matter across the entire field and let it break down to provide a rich, living soil which grows healthy plants. Cover crops get mowed and chopped, dropping nitrogen on the field. Then we cover

WE BREW COMPOST TEA TO ADD MICROORGANISMS TO THE
SOIL, ENHANCING OUR FIELDS AND GARDENS.

that with a layer of organic hay. The two together start the composting process, breaking down into fertilizer.

Our farm is a field nursery. We use organic fertilizers, which work more slowly than synthetics. That means our lilies take longer to grow than other nurseries' lilies. Because those other nurseries use synthetic fertilizers, they can grow plants faster and cheaper. But we think we have one up on them—we grow better plants.

It's not easy to see the difference between industrially produced plants and organically produced plants placed side by side. But it's easy to explain how the process affects people who buy plants. First, plants raised in good soil transition to a yard or garden more readily. So success for our customers is assured. Second, many nurseries pump plants full of substances we all try to minimize in everyday life, such as synthetic insecticides and fertilizers. Some of these things stay in plant tissue for months. Some lead to bee decline. Most are brimming with stuff you wouldn't even think about bringing into your kitchen—stuff I don't want to bring into my garden, much less into our bees' hives.

Organic management also means that we need more people. And a different type of worker. We love our local teens, nieces and nephews, sisters, and volunteers who keep us going. But we need students—interns who want to learn how to garden, how to make a living, and how to be in balance with the earth. Years ago, we established paid internships. Through connections with garden club ladies, college professors, and even accidental contacts from chance meetings on farms in Haiti, we've recruited a unique crew of interns.

Daddy would be proud.

Honestly, I don't know all of Daddy's motivations for his low-till farming. He was no hippy organic guy trying to change the world. He loved his old hand-crank Allis Chalmers tractor. Maybe he just didn't have money to buy a tiller. And maybe he couldn't afford the exterminators who wanted to remove the entire side of the house, kill the bees, and call in a plaster expert to rework the parlor ceiling. I don't recall Daddy's intentions. We don't know exactly what makes the bulbs come back each year, what makes the bees buzz, or what makes the interns show up. But Daddy had a respect for life and a love of young people. His actions started a transition that led us to where we are today—a beyond-organic farm where the balance of life, above and below ground, known and unknown, gets respect.

TOM'S BEES FEED ON EARLY FLOWERING ORANGE RIVER LILY
AND MAKE A DELICIOUS, FLORAL HONEY.

Bunnies in the Larkspur

May marks the real transition from spring to summer heat. On a May afternoon, it's easy to feel a little dread about the seriously high temperatures to come. But the few remaining cool days in May give a respite—a moment of wistfulness, almost hopefulness. The flowers of spring ephemerals like poppies, bachelor buttons, and larkspur seem so strong; it seems they could last all summer, despite their moniker. Ephemeral means "for a day, fleeting, transitory."

A new planting of larkspur *(Consolida ajacis)* starts out flowering as a mix of pink, white, and purple. Or sometimes a single selected color. In specialty seed catalogues, you can find some spiffy seed mixes, surely named by the same person who names paint colors: 'Frosted Skies', 'King Size Scarlet', 'Fancy Purple Picotee', or the weird plum one I like to call 'Week-Old Bruise'. There is a delicate white 'Snowcloud', too. But all slowly revert to blue. Larkspur always ends up making a sea of blue.

NO MATTER WHICH COLOR MIX YOU START WITH, LARKSPUR REVERTS TO
A HAPPY, EYE-CATCHING BLUE OVER TIME.

A little packet of seeds scattered at the right time grows into waist-high plants that seem to float above the ground, obscuring those pansies that have lasted since cold weather and tickling the blooms of tea roses. Larkspur covers unsightliness left by winter, too—old tools, broken fences, and rotting stumps that should be dealt with—but later. Slender stems are strong and stand up to spring rains and winds, to me wading through them to get a weed, and even to children getting their portraits made in the larkspurs' mist of blue.

There's always a bunny in the larkspur, too. Always. Each time I see larkspur, I remember Felder, my country-wise friend who first pointed out that bunny in the larkspur to me. I know that in May, no matter where that traveling jokester is, if he's with someone in the larkspur, he's going to get that surprised, whimsical look on his face and point out the bunny: "Oh my, look at that bunny in the larkspur! See him? No over this way. Let's sneak up on him. I'll show you." I won't spoil the ending. It's a fun surprise. We all end up duped, but we also love learning the secret when we finally see the bunny that lives in every larkspur flower.

When you see larkspur in a garden, stay with it, enjoy it, wade through it. But hold back from going out in May to buy it. October is the month for planting larkspur seeds in the South. On a cool rainy day, spread the seeds. Then watch the tiny leaves all winter, and enjoy the color mix in May. Afterward, watch the plants go to seed, dry up, and fade away. But that's not their end. They'll be back to start their cycle of rebirth in the fall. However, the next generation's flowers will be dominated by blue. It's just the way it is. No matter what color you originally buy, over the years, blue ends up dominating.

If you keep the plants happy and coming back long enough, your larkspur community changes in another way, too. It moves around the yard. Next year, it may all be in a totally different place from where you first planted it, as if the plants decided that next year they'd look better and bluer if they all came up on the other side of the path. In reality, what has happened is that the seeds got widely scattered. But some found a hospitable spot and survived in certain areas while others did not. Imagine larkspur in its home—the dry, rocky hills of Turkey. There, neither mulch nor summer rain touches the tough seeds. In the South, too much mulch or water from irrigation will make your larkspur seeds rot away.

Larkspur fills the gap of time between spring and summer flowers. By the end of May, as other joys of spring start to grab our attention, the larkspur blanket fades away and completely peters out with the rising heat of June. So take in that fairytale picture of larkspur-filled gardens and fields during this time. It's a beautiful, playful image and one that signals the end of spring. This ending, though, is a happy ending. Like that final watercolor painting in *The Velveteen Rabbit,* it promises the return of spring with its warm, sunny days and little blue bunnies hiding in the larkspur.

Mother's Day Field Open

In the woods, just down a dirt road, the families who established this community lie in a beautiful cemetery, draped with Spanish moss and contained by a crumbling brick wall. Many of them would have lived or visited on our little farm, which has long been a gathering place. Many of the women were gardeners, including Miss Bertha and others who taught me about flowers. On Mother's Day in the graveyard, their descendents have a cocktail party with their moms. They set up tents, chairs, and a bar under the China firs. I imagine more than a few splashes of gin and tonic get shared on the graves.

We have our own gathering, Mother's Day Field Open, on the lily farm. It's a sales day, a promotional day, and a reward day—a way to keep customers coming back and bringing friends. Anyone who's bought a bulb in the past or anyone on our e-mail list gets invited. And it's the day we introduce our new summer interns. It's also the first time that

ON MOTHER'S DAY, MULTIPLE GENERATIONS OF FAMILY AND
FRIENDS VISIT THE FARM.

those interns, newly released from school, learn how we organize a big event, and how we balance sales and personal connections. We celebrate all the things mothers and warm soil bring forth, starting with us, then great food, flowers, and stories about people. My mother Gloria is at the center of it all, having made this farm a gathering place for the past forty years.

Momma's earliest memories of her grandmother and of dirt always hold people's attention. One memory in particular makes Momma smile and seems to enthrall the young interns, too. As they gather around, Momma sets the scene. She's a little girl kneeling on the compacted gray earth of her grandmother's swept yard, reaching into a soft mound of dirt layered with pine straw. Her sweet southern lilt draws the young people further in, helping them to come face to face with something that they're all looking for but just can't quite name, some enchantment or feeling, some connection. Listen to Momma draw them in:

> "It was just magic to push my hands into the dark and feel around. I never knew what I'd come out with; I'd feel shapes and hunt for whatever we needed for supper. A potato! Out of the mound. It was such a joy and such a surprise to me as a little girl to *discover* it. Grandmother knew, of course. She'd grown the vegetables, layering potatoes, sweet potatoes, and turnips in this old mound of dirt and straw. We didn't have a refrigerator. We didn't have electricity. This is how we stored them, from frost until spring. They kept just fine layered in the dirt."

To build this storage mound, which would be called a potato clamp in Britain, Momma's Grandmother Tuten would dig out a circular pit, a foot deep or so, then layer into it potatoes and other vegetables with straw and dirt until it became a three-foot mound. The whole thing was protected from rain by a cone-shaped tin cap. The fact that Momma smiles at this memory of hard times tells us something about Grandmother Tuten and all those women in her life. They knew something practical. Poverty breeds resilience as well as reliance on tough, productive crops that store readily. Sweet potatoes grow without much care; they reliably yield pounds of nutritious food.

They also knew something powerful. They knew how to take the act of reaching into a dirt pile for supper and transform it into an adventure. Push your hands in and feel for certain shapes. Is that the one? How many more are there? How much magic could she make for a little girl? That's a skill my Momma learned well and uses often.

Momma's Grandmother Tuten lived a hard life in a hard place. Crocketville was and still is one of the poorest parts of South Carolina. Her husband tilled the garden in the spring with a mule, but otherwise, he didn't do much in the way of work. He mostly drank. He'd never gotten around to finishing the house, so it didn't even have glass in the windows. Grandmother Tuten had no tiller, no bagged fertilizer, no plastic hose, no pesticides. Those things didn't exist. Poor people made do.

Momma's father, my grandfather, farmed for other people. He owned the first tractor in Hampton County but no land, so he'd contract out himself and his tractor. But his death, when he was thirty-nine years old, left the family virtually homeless. They moved in with grandparents on the farm in Crocketville, an isolated spot made more so because the only transportation around was walking or catching a ride on a mule and wagon.

Yes, a mule-drawn wagon. I've heard her recount the stories to many young interns. Without self-pity or regret, she was just making conversation while she and the interns planted potatoes. But this wasn't the norm for the 1940s. By then, most farmers had a pickup. Privately, Momma has told me she was embarrassed by the mule cart. With interns though, she's making magic, connecting young people with the history of our food, our plants, and our dirt. To the interns, it all may seem like ancient history, something to google on their iPhone, but in reality, connections are what these young people are craving.

And they get them during our Mother's Day Field Open, when stories abundantly flow. The interns work beside Momma, help her lead tours, quickly getting up to speed on plant names, uses, and stories. A student intern from the University of Georgia once wrote down some of the stories, a sort of script that we could use for other tour days. That young woman, thoroughly engrossed, could tell the stories as if she'd lived them herself. It helps preserve the stories of thrusting a hand into a dirt pile to get a potato or visiting Henrietta Washington, the granddaughter of a freed slave woman whom Momma had checked in on in old age. And most of Momma's plants came from the strong women of her childhood, bits of Julia's dahlia, Urbana's pearl bush, and Henrietta Washington's rose.

This Mother's Day event is different from other Open Days in that visitors today are mostly women who arrive in multi-generational groups. Grandmothers, daughters, and grandchildren get connected to their past. We've had guests from Spokane, Washington to Wauchula, Florida. For some, poignant memories of their own family farms come rushing back when our mule brays. For others, it's all new, and we hope it grows into a new passion.

Mother's Day Field Open originally started to help show off our lilies and build our customer base. It has turned into much more. In fact, it's gotten pretty big, requiring pre-registration and coordinated check-out. It's our day to help the interns see the big picture. When they interview for their positions and when they work their first week, they tend to think that they're in for a slow summer full of weeding, digging lily bulbs, and making compost. When they've finished helping at the Mother's Day Field Open, they realize this farm stuff is a business—a personal family business that emphasizes the family part. These interns are employees, but in many ways, we treat them like family. No one does this better than Momma.

I'll never forget one night overhearing a conversation between Momma and a young Jay, a restless soul, a rolling stone who felt grounded on this lily farm, one of his few places of comfort. Still dirty from the workday and slightly drunk, he was unloading his anguish on Momma. He'd met the perfect woman. They were a great match in all ways. But as he talked, he started to cry.

"What's the problem then, Jay?" Momma asked.

"It can never work out, Mrs. Farmer. She's decided to turn into a man."

I wondered if I should intervene at that point. But without skipping a beat, Momma comforted him.

"Well, Jay, people do change, and maybe things will work out in a way you don't expect."

———————————

MOMMA (GLORIA FARMER) HAS MADE THE FARM A WELCOMING
GATHERING PLACE FOR THE PAST FORTY YEARS.

Our Sea of Pink

June's fields of flowers let everyone riding down the little dirt road know that this is a lily farm. It's pure indulgence, this sea of pink. We don't really need all those flowers for bulb production. After all, we're growing bulbs, not flowers. But they light up the pasture, fill the air with fragrance, moths and bees, and pleasure. And we get to share them. When our favorite and most floriferous crinum (*Crinum* 'Cecil Houdyshel') flowers en masse, we know it's summer. June starts off mild but changes soon enough to real summer—buckets of rain

JUNE'S GLORIOUS FIELD OF *CRINUM* 'CECIL HOUDYSHEL' SIGNALS THAT
RELENTLESS HEAT WILL SOON BE UPON US.

most afternoons, nights when the temperature is the same at midnight as it was after the afternoon rain, and everything growing wild. June is kind of crinum crazy.

Although I associate crinum with the Deep South, crinum had a heyday in California in the early 1900s. Luther Burbank, a friend of inventor Thomas Edison, was one of America's most successful horticulturists. A pop icon of the day, Burbank hybridized hundreds of the food plants that we eat today, and he also hybridized crinum. His contemporary, a nurseryman named Cecil Houdyshel, bred crinum, too. Both are said to have received crinum from a huge collection shipped from India in 1900. These turn-of-the-century horticulturists inspired a younger generation of Americans to collect crinum.

That next generation, a competitive lot, became my mentors. Mostly World War II fellas, they loved to one-up each other. They'd left the farms as boys, seen the world in war, and come back as men who intended to change things. One of them decided the antique variety, the full soft-pink crinum 'Peachblow', could be better. After years of work, he named his creation 'Improved Peachblow'. These hybridizers always strove to create plants that were rare and new and better and expensive. Patrick Malcolm, the horticulturist who added "Improved" to Peachblow, helped me get started growing my first crinum crop. I remember him standing in his field wearing a tissue-thin madras shirt and big straw hat and waist-deep in pink Cecil flowers. Tire-track roads wound through his lily fields. The summer was hot and the field was buggy. It used to be a pecan grove, so there was a bit of relief under the trees' light shade. He—Mr. Malcolm to me—knew the rare and unique, and he knew that nothing would work as well as *Crinum* 'Cecil Houdyshel' to get me, the next generation, hooked. He helped me decide that Cecil should be my first big investment, my starter crinum.

Those first crates I purchased from him, a $500 investment, were a huge commitment for me at the time. It was a mortgage payment. There was no real demand for crinums then. No one wrote glossy magazine articles about crinums. To get a return on my investment would take cultivating and learning how to awaken a market. And patience, too. There would be no instant gratification.

They didn't sell well at first, but those crinum didn't care. They did their thing and grew. Boy, did they grow! We soon had rows and rows of pink flowers, then a whole field of them. Crinum are stunning all day but pure magic comes at dusk. It's the time when the drooping new buds start to raise themselves up, to inflate. By dark, new flowers are fully open, releasing their sweet powdery perfume. In the gloaming (I love that word.), the target audience for this extravagant scented display shows up. The moths arrive. This sea of pink, this cloud of nighttime perfume, is all about sex. Crinum flowers are specially adapted for moth pollination, the term is *sphingophilous,* referring to a specific family of moths. *Sphingophilous.* I love that word, too, probably as much as the hawkmoths love Cecil.

A better businessman might say this field of flowers represented a failure to launch.

It's exactly the opposite. There's so much launching, so many new moth babies being made in this field at night, we all deserve a bottle of champagne. I'm always the creative businessman, and I say this field is sex appeal. People tiptoe out there, hunker down a bit, and take selfies shoulder-deep in the pink trumpets. It's our storefront and the Instagram moment no photographer can resist.

But the Cecil field in flower is more than a moment for me. It's part of a kaleidoscope of thousands of shiny June moments. Hovering moths in the evenings—full, puffed-up, and pouring perfume into full-moon nights. Mornings at full mast—drops of dew clinging to buds and leaves. Warm ground—soft and perfect for bare feet. Coffee break photos—maybe one with big lavender balls of elephant garlic in the background. T-shirts coming off for afternoon work—letting me feel those flowers on my skin as I reach down to dig.

As glorious as Cecil is in June, we still have to dig the plants out and send them on their way. The whole plant—leaves, flowers, and bulbs—gets laid out and chopped back. Leaves to the burn pile, bulbs to the shipping shed, flowers into old buckets. We can't bear to waste the flowers, so they go to Momma's church or to friends in city apartments. Even cut and in a vase, Cecil still follows its cycle of puffing up and releasing perfume in the evening, then opening wide for the morning light and staying big and pink all June long.

A YOUNG FATHER KNEELS DOWN TO TAKE A SELFIE IN THE
PINK SEA OF *CRINUM* 'CECIL HOUDYSHEL' FLOWERS.

Fathers and Nice Packages

Frank Dunaway gave my sister a piglet for her 16th birthday. He was courting her. He was apparently not trying to impress our daddy, whose eyes, behind photogray glasses with side angle protectors, got all red and veiny, his temples bulged, and gray hair rolled like thunder clouds. He spoke clearly, precisely, from somewhere deep in his gut. "What kind of a fool?" He had to take a deep breath and sigh break, "What kind of a fool gives a pig as a present?" Had Daddy been in a cartoon, those words would have loomed in large and dark capital letters in a bubble over his head. He needed a slow, side-to-side head shake and a few seconds to wipe sweat from his crew cut before he said, "Good God Almighty, take it back and I don't mean tomorrow."

Fathers used to be direct and demanding that way. But today's fathers, the young ones who show up at our Farm Open on Father's Day, would say something sweet about the pig

---

YOUNG FATHERS COME OUT WITH CHILDREN AND PARENTS ON OUR
FARM OPEN ON FATHER'S DAY.

gift or at least counsel young Frank about his present-giving skills. Many of them today, I think we'd agree, would be gentler in their words, not reacting like Daddy did.

We encourage farm visits from these young fathers and their families. We want them to use those nurturing skills to teach their families and to build a lifelong gardening hobby that becomes a connection to the earth and a bridge to other generations.

Older guys also come out, retired from amazing careers and now pursuing an already developed gardening hobby. They come solo or with friends. One said to me, "I played golf and racketball for years. Will you teach me to garden? I need something creative and something I can do at home while the smoker is going." I take that as a vulnerable question from a man seeking meaning in life. It's also a compliment beyond compare. I not only helped him pick plants from our fields but also ended up designing his yard and planting it with him, including a fig tree because fig wood makes a super sweet glaze on smoked pork loin.

The older guys have time to commit, to hang around and to indulge in our gardens, barns, and farm work. However, the young fathers come out with children, on a quick Saturday-morning field trip. They may not spend as much time, but they have a way of making it matter. They get enthralled with parsley and peppers in the vegetable garden or the donkey-poo compost pile. They tell a story to relate these things to their children, usually via food. "Remember when you planted flowers with Grandpa and he had that bag of good black dirt?" They make connections. What better way for a child, and father, to learn? These young men teach in nurturing ways fathers a generation or two back didn't or couldn't.

My mind wanders back to my daddy. He taught me tons of stuff: barn work, building chimneys, how rattlesnakes smell like goats, caring for calves and pigs. He could do anything. He established a scholarship fund for the Beech Island Agricultural Club. He whistled like the River Kwai crew. He was part of the Navy Construction Battalion, the Seabees who built Guantanamo Bay for goodness sakes. I realize that his teaching me to do stuff was his type of nurturing, but it didn't feel nurturing at the time. While we were doing whatever we were doing, he'd get frustrated if I couldn't do it perfectly. Fixing up this dilapidated farm with little money and only children as helpers had to have been frustrating. Having a soft son must have been, too.

But these nurturing young dads raise children the way I raise plants—with patience and individual understanding. I want them to raise plants at home, too, so their children continue to learn connections between plants, food, health, and nurturing men. I want them to hang around as clients, too.

For any small business, understanding new customers leads to long-term customers, which leads to long-term success. We pay attention to who attends our farm events and when. We've learned, for instance, that Father's Day events should start early and end early. Guys come in the morning for a brief road trip then they head out to the next stop—totally different from the lingering gatherings on Mother's Day.

In their short visit, we want visitors to have more than just pictures on the phone. Our customers get lessons to go. Since we sell bare root bulbs, something unfamiliar to many people, we have to provide detailed, explicit instructions to ensure success. For those who do buy a plant or bulb, my partner Tom works especially hard to send them home with all the information they'll need to know to plant their new crinum lily.

Tom gets all that sort of stuff readied in the crinum shed, that old chicken house that's now our shipping shed. Outside, it's clad in open corn-crib siding—a faded rainbow of old boards. The Regina's Disco Lounge sign and the acrylic chandelier hang under a tin roof on the front. That little chicken house is quirky and colorful with its interior paint job: splatters of orange, blue, and yellow. Despite all that, there's a real efficiency to its new shipping-shed layout. Tom, trained as an architectural draftsman years ago, laid out the inside of the small, multi-function building for smooth workflow. Make no mistake. This is no typical shipping shed. It's unique—funky with a link to heritage. It gets your attention. And it sets the tone for Tom as he shares planting instructions, notes, and bulbs. In short, this resurrected chicken house is where Tom shares our farm. This is Tom's sharing shed.

Tom wants the packages that contain the bulbs we sell to inspire. Like his sharing shed, he wants them to set the tone for the planting experience. Tom understands that people

TOM AND CONNELLY WANT PEOPLE TO FEEL LIKE THEY'RE OPENING A
GIFT WHEN THEY RECEIVE A PACKAGE OF BULBS FROM THE FARM.

need some motivation. Planting a big crinum bulb can be intimidating—the reason it's easy for some people to procrastinate. Tom has compassion for those folks, and his natural instinct is to send them on their way with useful information and a clear sense of direction. He gets those qualities from his dad, a military veteran who became a policeman in civilian life. It wasn't unusual for Tom to hear from high school friends that his dad had pulled them over with beer and weed. They were scared to death. But several told Tom later they hadn't been charged. Tom's dad had told them to dump the contraband, straighten up, and go home this time. He believed in providing guidance and opportunity for learning.

Tom continues the tradition with the useful information that he puts into each lily box he ships. Tom deepens the connection with each customer by making the package feel like a gift. He begins with the crinum bulb itself, carefully cleaning it and trimming the brown roots and leaves. Then he assembles instructions, including our photo and a storybook that explains how to plant the bulb. Next he rolls the bulb and a cushion of excelsior into a corrugated tube. He ties it all together with jute baling twine and writes a personal note on the invoice. The package opens like a gift.

Putting this kind of attention into a package is a part of Tom's Japanese heritage. As a child, Tom fondly recalls helping his war-bride mother open packages mailed from friends and department stores in Japan. Persimmons, magazines, but mostly cloth for his mom to use to make her clothes—all packed with precision, every corner folded perfectly and tied with an easy-to-untie string. When talking about Japan, his mom recalled that in each checkout line, stores had a designated person to expertly wrap packages for customers. So anyone walking out of the store went home with their purchase efficiently and beautifully wrapped.

About once a month, someone who has received a package from the farm takes the time to get in touch with Tom. They send a handwritten letter in response to Tom's personal note and the love that he put into their package of bulbs. People feel it; this package is more than a brown box from a warehouse, it's from a sharing shed.

On this hot Father's Day afternoon, after everyone has gone, I imagine people at home opening their boxes. I imagine they notice the paper, the note, and the gift-like presentation. I imagine them dreaming of where this bulb will grow and how nurturing will turn it into a flowering family heirloom.

It's been a long day. My mind returns to Daddy and the pig. I still recall my tough-on-the-outside Daddy watching that little pig trundle through dry clover as he found a place to squat and pee. "Look'a'there, fella hasn't even learned to pee like a boy pig yet. Y'all know we have to make him a stall away from the grown pigs for a while. They'll hurt him." Daddy's heart swelled for that vulnerable creature. He might even have teared up behind the photogray lenses thinking about what our nurturing would bring.

But nothing lasts forever. That piglet present grew into something the whole family loved. Bacon.

Spider Lily Flick

Protected from searing sun by a big straw hat, I'm crouched in the field, kind of in my own little world. Spider lily leaves stand almost erect, but they arch enough to block my view, and their pointy white flower buds would poke me in the eye if I looked up suddenly. Tough spider lilies with their beautiful, fragile genus name, *Hymenocallis,* look like a smaller, tidier version of crinum. Their flowers are more delicate, their flowering period briefer. We have only one row of them, and I'm crouched there in my weeding position on a sweltering July afternoon. I stand up to stretch. After a tiny swoon in my head, my old eyes slowly focus on the blurred scene beyond the fenced flower fields.

In a sea of green pasture, a swayback, whitish donkey stands belly-deep in uncut grass. Way across the pasture, an orange tractor mows in straight lines, leaving behind walkable mown turf, which will provide space for wedding guests to park their cars tomorrow. Ahead of the tractor stands the shaggy soft meadow. And above, wedding-dress white egrets soar. A few of them tiptoe in the cut grass.

Those egrets strut by, pulling their bodies back a bit while thrusting their heads forward, pointing, stalking, ready to lance their prey. They move mechanically like robots, a stark contrast to their graceful flights. When their wings spread, I get a glimpse of the cotton-candy puffs of under-wing feathers. These African cow egrets have the same ethereal feathers of their American cousins—feathers so desired for ladies hats that Victorians almost caused their extinction.

The hot, humid summer is when the egrets come. They migrate through, pasture to pasture. We call them cowbirds. We don't have cows anymore. But the egrets seem happy with that portly old donkey named Buck.

Buck would be pristine white except that he likes to roll in a certain bare spot. I guess he thinks the turmeric-colored clay works like bug repellant. The result is that he's usually more off-orange than white. Two lucky egrets perch on his back, but Buck is oblivious to his riders. He grazes slowly and methodically. Always. He's a laid-back vegetarian, an unwitting hunting perch for the military precision of the meat-seeking birds. Their sleek simple lines and purity of color belie a brutal appetite for mice and toads. As the tractor mows, little critters suddenly become exposed and scamper and hop for cover. Egrets flock to hunt during mowing, stabbing a toad, tossing it up in the air, catching it, and packing their gullets full of their prey.

What led to this moment is an ironic backstory of decaying grass and weeds. Decay

---

SOME NATURAL GLUE, POSSIBILITY, AND TENSION HOLD TOGETHER
DELICATE MEMBRANES OF HYMENOCALLIS.

brings life. Insects breed and grow, then die and rot in the duff. In this way, insects become frogs and mice. Mice become egrets. Egrets become the fluff of ladies' hats and stylized icons on fountains. The boy driving the tractor seems unaware. His camo BMX cap points straight ahead toward his goal—the fence on the other side of the pasture and getting-off time. Tomorrow's wedding party will march right across this grass aiming toward the big I-do moment under the magnolia tree. But here's the thing that captivates me so much: The farm fella driving the tractor right now doesn't get his part in this story. All those wedding guests won't get how life is changing below their feet as they witness the life-changing vows taking place in front of them. I easily get drawn into pondering all of that, watching the boy on his tractor cutting grass and weeds in the field.

It's time to get back to work. I finish taking in the scene and crouch again into weeding.

In July, crabgrass sprawls from a single central node like a giant toy spider or a crab. It spreads its legs and sort of floats over the spider lily leaves. So when I select the right central stalk and pull, a bunch comes out at once. I get the satisfaction of seeing a messy area cleaned quickly. One precise crabgrass pull produces an area the size of a card table that is suddenly clean and tidy. Voilà! Sometimes crabgrass decides to grow low and flat, I leave those alone. Soon enough, those low, flat ones will be covered up by sprawling black-eyed pea vines.

Peas, planted as a cover crop, thrive in our summer rain and heat, smothering low weeds. Pea vines make natural, green, and free mulch. After frost, the pea vines rot and break down to become part of our soil fertility system. Sometimes we mow them as part of our sheet compost practice. They add to the soil nitrogen that our plants use. The pea duff also feeds the insects. It's all one interconnected system that includes a boy on a tractor, a bride and groom, birds and bugs, egrets and lilies.

Some plants can't tolerate the sprawling grass nor the smothering peas. Short and thin spider lily leaves need exposure to sun. Starting in early July, their beautifully curved white flowers stretch upward on thin necks. A greenish-white spear emerges, perfectly pointed like the egret's beak. Twisted petals remain fused at the tip. During the late part of the day, petals inflate and try to get themselves unfused. As the sun dips behind the trees, the petals have made a cage of thin curved white bars. Given their delicate construction, the spider lilies' twilight opening ought to be graceful. They should dance like Ginger Rogers. But like those elegant egrets with their herky-jerky hunting walk, spider lilies open with startling snaps. One petal thrusts out here. Another flicks apart over there. You have to be there at just the right moment to see the awkward robotic opening transform, in only a minute, into petals held upward in perfect symmetry with tiny yellow beacons at the center. That's also when the flowers release seductive fragrances, enticing all sorts of night moths to stick their heads in, to pollinate, to be a part of that story of one thing becoming another. If I'm ever a little bored on a July evening, after the big sun hat hangs on a hook and after a shower, I open a beer and head to the spider lily row to watch the tiny moths on the unfurling flowers.

You know, that might seem kind of sad, like a really boring life for a guy—hanging out in the crinum field on a July night to watch moths and flowers. But for me, for moths and spider lilies, that's *the* moment. It's life.

WHITE SPIDER LILIES REVEAL THEIR ELEGANCE IN LATE AFTERNOON, ENTICING NOCTURNAL MOTHS TO POLLINATE.

A Three T-shirt Day

July is just hot. All day. All night. I love it.

This is burning weather for hosta and hollyhocks and rotting days for dianthus and digitalis. But our heat-needing plants jump. Crinum, peanuts, okra, sugar cane, lantana, princess flower, frog fruit, and that jade vine that made only a wimpy little trunk through June—they all need weekly machete work by the end of July.

Black-eyed pea seeds that dropped on the ground last season germinate and start to climb over the crinum. We plant sweet potato slips and new crinum seedlings now. They're the kind of plants that love—no, need—humidity and constantly heating up soil.

In July, some people retreat to the lake, the mountains, or the nearest a/c. But I feel right and connected through the hot, heavy, humid air. These are three-T-shirt days. By the first work break at 9:30 a.m., number one is done. By lunch, number two gets draped

---

SHADE FROM THE PECAN TREES OFFER RELIEF FROM THE
HOT, HAZY DAYS OF JULY.

over a bush in the sun. By the afternoon break, if it didn't rain and give those T-shirts that funky mildew smell, it's time to start over with number one. Look at it this way: The water content of cells—ours, crinum, peanuts, and dogs sleeping under the truck—connects all those cell parts. That floating haze of 98 percent humidity connects us in the same way. It means we're all one.

OK. That may be a little too poetic for some. I do love the heat and humidity at moments, but I know that heat dehydrates and gives me kidney stones. It makes me see the world through sweat and mud-smudged lenses. I can still revel in being drenched and dirty because I love sub-tropical plants, especially the late-flowering crinum lilies that only start to flower now. Hate it. Love it. Thrive in it. Retreat from it. Any way you want to put it, I love my cold water shower at the back of the barn and slow July afternoons in the shade.

It's also the time of year when there's nothing like a good road trip in an air-conditioned truck. July is a great time to explore, but unlike people who like to escape to cool climes, I seek more heat and the plants that thrive in it. These days, we take interns and young employees along on our road trips so they can learn the public gardens and natural landscapes of south Georgia and Florida.

Back in the '80s, a man named Jim Porter took me to meet a national network of serious crinum collectors like Les Hannibal, the man who wrote the first "bible of crinum." Jim and I took long crinum-collecting road trips—Miami, New Orleans, San Antonio—and visited breeders like Texan Marcelle Sheppard. You get to know people on road trips. Jim was a retired teacher known around town as Mr. Porter. He was a Saturday Gamecock football fan, a Sunday morning Baptist, and he seemed the ultimate conservative. Other than crinum, we had little in common. Jim never met a stranger, and he knew the hobbyists and the backwoods breeders, too. He could turn on country charm and talk us into any garden we drove past. On one of those long road trips through Florida, Jim asked me if we could spare an evening for an Aerosmith concert in Tampa, confiding that Steven Tyler's ambiguous gender and sexuality had intrigued him for years. What the hell? I didn't see that coming, and I didn't want to go to that concert with him. I steered that conversation back to plants.

Eventually, we pulled into a trailer park in the scrubby pine woods outside of Gainesville to visit a young bulb-growing friend of his. The gardener, a big-haired country girl about my age, told me in confidence, "You know that man saved me. I was from that awful mill village in Columbia (South Carolina). The other boys picked on me. Almost killed me. He was my teacher. He paid for me to leave to become who I am today."

Jim kept connected to all these crinum lovers, experts, and experimenters all over the country. Back then it was sort of like a secret society—no cell phones, no appointments, just paper maps and a common interest when people would drop whatever they were doing to share their crinum stories. So July means road trips, and road trips mean making connections and comparisons and seeing the truth in each other through flowers.

On the farm, in between road trips, we get a lot of work done in and around the heat. A typical day goes something like this. Dawn means coffee and protein shake. Gotta eat lite in the heat. Early hours before the sun broils mean digging bulbs or similar physical work like dividing, spreading compost, or getting brush off fences. We keep a giant orange water cooler under a shed and make frequent trips between there and the fields during the work day. We have only small paper cups at the water cooler. There's a reason for that, too. It keeps people coming back to the water cooler, to the shade, encouraging frequent drinks and breaks from the sun. Of course, it also reduces trash because we write our names on the cups and reuse them.

After lunch the pace slows, but it's not languid by any means. We do things like weeding, irrigation repair, sharpening tools, and taking inventory. We also do our evaluations, comparisons, and our curation work. We evaluate new crinum cultivars procured from friends or reliable nurseries and today's young breeders. We also look at mix-ups or naming problems. Sometimes that means we've lost a tag. But sometimes it means someone else has caused confusion by putting a new marketing name on an old plant. For example, the plant with the cumbersome name 'Menehune' was dubbed Purple Rain a while back. It's a nice idea, but you can't just go around renaming things. It's like someone deciding to rename you to try to improve your image. So on July afternoons, we curate. We take the time to make notes, take photographs, and make side-by-side comparisons. We also text and use the Facebook group *Crinum Lovers* to share information with people who appreciate clarity around naming issues. These digital platforms also provide a place where we can all show off our flowers. We try very hard to make certain that we grow and offer our customers only properly named plants—and only the best of the best.

I'm particular about reds. In my opinion, there are too many and too many similar to each other. Since July brings all the so-called reds into flower, I track flowering time, sturdiness, size differences, duration, and fragrance among them. If I can't tell the difference, they don't make our cut. Recently, I've culled out 'Magenta', 'Burgundy', and 'This Is Outrageous'. Those reds don't stand up or stand out when compared to the old standard, a red that a 1930s Florida plantsman came up with and named for his wife, Ellen Bosanquet.

This sort of evaluation becomes our research. It's part of what makes our farm a horticultural experiment station. It's what keeps us serious and keeps me connected to my career of building serious public gardens—places where plants connect people and give them that "aha" moment.

On a sultry July morning a group of truly dedicated master gardeners shows up for the last of our summer tours. Their bus windows drip and fog up because of the contrast between the a/c inside and the humidity outside. They swarm out of the bus and head straight to the water cooler. Soon enough, their paper cups soak up so much water from both the inside and the outside that they start to crumple. In their master gardener classes, they've learned the conventional wisdom of horticulture that says it's best to plant perennials in fall or winter, when root growth gets the plant ready for summer stress. So they're surprised to learn that we plant crinum all summer. It makes perfect sense that plants which come from places without cold can be planted all summer long. I love when they get this, when they have that "aha" moment. This is a tiny lesson, easy to share, that can have a big impact for them. We continue the farm tour looking for more lessons. We walk mostly on the shady paths, and I suggest that we're all one, cellularly connected through the cytoplasm of that 98 percent humidity. They laugh, but I'm serious. We are internally connected just as we connect externally through our appreciation of plants. They laugh even more when I suggest they stay after lunch, for a hands-on lesson pulling subtropical weeds.

Oh, well. I try.

MY MENTOR AND FRIEND JIM PORTER STIMULATED MY PASSION FOR CRINUM. HE ALSO INTRODUCED ME TO THE OLDER GENERATION OF COLLECTORS AND CRINUM BREEDERS.

By August, the towering, hairy okra plants can be more
than intimidating, even for Momma.

Soulful Okra

Boiled in chicken broth, slimy, pickled, or cast-iron-fried—even when half the batter comes off—I love okra. It's not just for supper anymore either. Wide, soft yellow flowers, held high, add summer color to ornamental gardens. Hollyhock-like leaves bring texture. Sturdy, thick stems offer climbing beans a place to run up, working two crops into one space. Creative people paint the pods for Christmas decor. Okra pods store well and germinate quickly, and the plant grows so fast that it easily captures attention.

I realized only recently that okra is so much a southern thing that some Americans have never tried it. That's hard for me to believe. Do you know that song about millions of peaches? I think that the '90s band, The Presidents of the United States, should do a follow-up to it. The lyrics could be like:

> Movin' to the country,
> Gonna eat a lot of okras…
> Millions of okras, okras for me,
> Millions of okras, okras for free.

Did I mention that I really like okra?

We seed in okra and let it grow up right next to the rows of lilies. It gets tall, like broomsticks or bamboo, foresting over the lilies. We get started in June by soaking the BB-sized seeds in water for twenty-four hours. Then we direct sow those in the hot soil, and okra plants come right up in leaps and bounds. And in July, we always think something's wrong. We always think the okra are not growing enough. Are they ever going to fruit? We're ready for our "millions of okras"!

Suddenly those plants jump from knee high to shoulder high. By mid-August, every meal at the farm house includes those hairy little stars, and we know for real the dog days of summer have arrived. Okra means August.

In addition to the regular hairy-pod veggie that okra fans know and love, we also grow a few odd okras. There's the version that I call "showy okra"—the kind that likes to put on airs, trying to tart itself up by having showy red flowers. It's really called ambrette and is valued for its micronutrient content in India. Ambrette's toasted seeds become perfume, candy, and a flavor in Benedictine, a French liqueur. The version with huge yellow flowers is called manihot or sunset hibiscus. It's commonly served as cooked greens in Malaysia and is used to make paper in Japan. We just like its flowers and appreciate how easy it is to share as seeds or cuttings that can be planted directly in the ground. Every single part of okra has a medicinal, nutritional, or essential oil use. Okra has soul.

If I had a small city garden and could only grow one veggie, it would be okra. It takes no care, attracts no pest, and makes a lot of food. I've never had to spray an okra plant or tell someone how to grow it. Okra just grows and grows. It requires only that you stay on top of harvesting it every other day. Otherwise, its fruit production slows. And we sure don't want okra to slow down.

Peak okra season makes me a little sad inside though. I know what it means. The earth is turning. Fall is coming.

It seems that okra has always been a part of my life. Usually it was fried at our house. I didn't know this was anything but normal. Then when I was in graduate school in chilly Washington state, I was shocked that no one seemed to know about okra in Seattle. I complained about that, but no one listened. One day an acquaintance was excited to take me to a secret dive of a restaurant. He said it was a soul food place. I had no idea what that meant. It wasn't a food term we used on our farm. I was even more confused when we were served fried okra, catfish, and cornbread. "Wait!" I said. "This is my Momma's cooking. Is this soul food?" I'd grown up on this stuff and never realized that I was eating dishes cultivated in the kitchens of Gullah women.

Okra cakes is another way we ate okra. I love okra cakes. They're a really eggy, puffy pan-fried corn bread with chopped okra—something between a hoe cake and an omelet. Then there's stewed okra. It's somewhat slimy and probably has a lot to do with the bad rap okra sometimes gets. But it's mighty tasty. I had okra stew one time in Haiti. It had whole thumb-sized pods floating in a thin garlicky beef broth and was served over rice. And, of course, Momma pickles okra. One summer she and her friend Sara put up about 100 quarts. That's a lot of pickled okra! We ended up donating a lot of it to an awards lunch for environmentally friendly politicians.

As much as I liked to eat okra, I didn't like to pick it. I thought picking okra amounted to a form of corporal punishment on the farm. Instead of restriction or getting a spanking, picking okra was a punishment for us as teenagers. "You forgot to take out the trash? Then do it now and go pick the okra, too!" I still don't like to pick it. Here's why. Okra gets tall, and when you reach up into it, its hairs get into the tender skin on the underside of your forearms. There are two ways to deal with this. The obvious is to wear a shirt. The less obvious is to apply a pruning technique called ratooning. This simple technique requires that you chop the entire plant back to about a foot tall, then give it a little extra water and fertilizer. By fall, you will have a handsome bushy plant with easy-to-reach pods.

Of course, some people don't mind having tall okra plants. For people with back and knee issues, reaching down to work with the many low-growing veggies is not an easy thing. Okra is perfect for Momma and her friends. Okra is perfect for being outside during the early mornings of summer. It's perfect for picking and talking.

The thick sweltering heat of August may seem overwhelming to most of us, but okra loves the heat. These scorching August days are like those in Africa, its ancestral home. I bet there—let's face it everywhere—smart people get out in the okra patch in the coolness of the morning, at the crack of dawn and the rising of the sun. To this day, okra makes me think of cool sunrises at home and Momma's morning mantra, "I'm going to cut the okra before it gets too hot."

BEAUTIFUL OKRA FLOWERS LOOK LIKE THEIR COUSINS, THE HIBISCUS. BOTH ARE IN THE MALLOW FAMILY.

Country-Boy Death Doula

I killed today. In the eye-searing August sunshine. I killed. No, that's not quite right. I helped something die. It's the darkest, heaviest job you do on a farm.

Daddy taught us to shoot. We would shoot at soup cans on fence posts, paper-plate bullseyes on hay bales, and old bottles. Bottles were the best because they shattered. It was instant gratification for us, but Daddy said the broken glass would always be there—that shards would rise to the surface, and one day maybe years from now, we'd be out here barefoot and get cut.

We shot crows, too. They used to come to the farm in noisy black clouds, stealing pounds of nuts and taking away the only income we had in the fall and winter. Crows love pecans, but city people do, too. So we sold nuts in five- and ten-pound packages made from brown paper grocery bags. We charged a quarter a pound. In the cool days before Thanksgiving when pecan leaves were all brown and wet, covering the nuts on the ground, we'd have crow-shooting contests to see who could kill the most. That sort of competition never really interested me, but the reason for it seemed justified. I could understand why we needed to kill crows. We needed to protect our livelihood.

Then one wet morning, that all changed. I shot a crow and went over to where she fell. Instead of a black crow, I found an iridescent rainbow creature. At first I thought some tropical bird had flown through our field and I'd killed her. She was glorious and limp. I knew her head would loll over if I tried to pick her up. The thought paralyzed me, and I couldn't make myself pick up her body, that beanbag of dead beautiful. For whatever reason—maybe for comfort, maybe out of shame—I went to get Daddy. The crow was gone when we came back. We looked all over but couldn't find her. To this day, I still see her in all her vivid shiny color, and my throat aches.

For one more summer, the one after that rainbow crow revelation, I was a hunter. Then, trying to reconcile and compromise, I became a stalker. Barefoot and with my cat companion, the two of us were as careful as Cherokees moving quietly through the magnolia swamp. We became familiar with the canopy and the architecture of the swamp, the movement of trees, the light and shadows. We knew which animals came out at dawn, which ones at dusk. We even climbed, perched and tracked from the treetops. This might all sound sort of country-boy butch, but it was not that at all. Picture this: a skinny pre-teen in cut-off jeans with a bag made of woven upholstery fabric that I'd sewn myself and slung over a bare shoulder. My gun was a sawed-off .22-caliber rifle. I loved it because Daddy told me the story of running over it with a bulldozer when he was eighteen, then spending an afternoon with an old blacksmith who helped him cut it and true it up.

Hunting squirrels, I was supposed to look up, but I didn't always. I'd stop to dig up ferns and little honeysuckle azaleas and stuff them into my bag with squirrel tails. My hunting companion ate the bodies while I got the tails. She was not a real pointer. She wasn't even a dog. She was a big fluffy cat named Alexania for my Great Aunt Xania, who was tough, wiry, and outspoken in contrast to the Confederate luxury she'd been born into. She was said to be the youngest school teacher ever in South Carolina. I remember being served by really old black women at Xania's dining room table and being instructed on utensils: "Young ladies and gentlemen use a napkin to pat their lips. Do not wipe. Pat. Pat. Pat." And I remember her leading us children through her swept yard, hunting for buckeyes. She said we should keep them for our wedding day. A groom should always have a buckeye in his pocket for luck. I thought of her the day Tom and I got married in our bathing suits, at a solar eclipse pool party—no pockets, no buckeyes, but a tiny flicker of guilt that I didn't follow Aunt Xanias advice. I wonder how she would have felt about having a cat named for her.

My Alexania could move through dry leaves like a rattlesnake with never a sound. She was evenly colored, perfectly camouflaged against the big tan magnolia leaves and black swamp mud. Alexania the Huntress was so dedicated that she'd even get her feet wet if necessary. She'd watch for a squirrel to fall, eat it in minutes, leave me the tail, and tiptoe away, leading me toward the next course. I tried to watch treetops diligently, hunting mostly for the cat while learning to see and feel and to be part of the web of the woods.

Besides my quiet stalking days, there was enough death on the farm to keep me from seeking other hunting trips. Aunt Xania died soon after her old husband, Oregon, whom I remember only in a wooden rocking chair on the porch. He had white hair, and he was frail, barely thicker than the rocking chair cushions. He was really old, Confederate-veteran old when he died. Sometime after Xania and Oregon died, my huntress cat Alexania disappeared. Farm cats go away to die. They just go away. My dog Lady, who people said was "soft" or afraid of gun noises, got kicked by a cow. She whimpered, bloated, and died under the house.

My squirrel stalking eventually came to an end. It was all about the woods anyway. And maybe about being alone with the creatures who wanted me, barefoot and part of the earth. I never liked to kill as a group sport and didn't like hunting trips with the other boys. I never felt part of the group. No deer camp trips for me. What if they saw through me, found out I was shaken by death? "Sissy Jenks! Look! The sissy's crying over a six-pointer." I knew myself and the truth hurts. I cried enough over dead chicks—golfball-sized, pewter-colored guinea chicks with elegant little curved beaks. I saw them peek out first thing in the morning before school. Perfectly balanced, wind-up toys, spilling out from beneath the hen, all eager to explore the world under the rose bushes. By the afternoon they were a red muddy mess with bloody holes pecked into their skulls by the male, the cock. In less than eight hours, they were all dead.

When I was sent to the city for high school, I met urban teens who liked to hunt on weekends. They had gun magazines, portable deer stands, and camo everything. They even wore Duckhead pants and blue rubber "duck shoes" to school but went to the woods only on Saturday mornings. I'd been in the woods too much, killed too much, been dirty and itchy too often. I wanted to get away to the city to be with the new-wave invaders and social deviants at the *Rocky Horror Picture Show* and in the Athens love shacks that the B-52s sang of. It was the '80s, and Athens was the center of the alt-rock music scene. I wanted city pleasures: lights at night, queer bars, and slam dances. So I had to make two lives. I put my John Deere cap over my yellow Mohawk and a Band-Aid over my earrings when I went back to the farm—which was every day. It all seemed fairly normal to me, but at some level, I knew it would end.

I danced away from the woods, from too many layers of history, from the farm, family, and the cycles of nature. I sought out cities full of creative people, where self-expression reigned—Seattle, grad school, and the grunge scene. In that city life, one important farm skill was needed again. Friends would ask me to take care of urban problems like a rabbit in the garden, a possum in the basement, a sick old urban rooster, or even an occasional suburban goat. I remember every aching body, lolling head, open mouth, and final heavy breath.

And I soon realized that these skills would be needed with friends. It was the height of the AIDS epidemic. I remember one specific moment with my once buff boyfriend, a Midwestern corn-fed fella. When we moved in together, he'd just posed as Mr. June in the Leatherman's calendar, clad in leather with muscles bulging. One morning a few months later, I found him sprawled out on the kitchen floor unable to get up. Wasting they called it—skin and bones like Uncle Oregon. I got down on the floor with him. We laughed a minute then fell into a full-on, throat-swelling sadness as we wept for the brevity of our time together. He would put on a determined face for everyone else but would feel safe enough to admit fear and anger with me. I think some of that farm training helped me understand. He was the first dying person I'd been with. His death was the first time I realized that the compassion, guidance, and comfort I learned from animal deaths on the farm could translate to people. His death was the first of many to come. In the mid '80s, boys like me who ran to the city to escape farm life (and death) found a generation of men just a few years older than we were. They were our mentors, our trailblazers. They were men who had left the farms earlier than we did. They were the men who fought and demanded and made a whole new world for us to live in. They were also the men who needed us to help them die.

Many deaths later, I remember most clearly the eyes of my father as he lay on the emergency room gurney. His eyes locked on mine, gentle and terrified, pleading for release and strength and permission. I gave that permission: "You can go. I'll take care of things here as you taught me to. No more suffering. Thank you. Go on now. I'll grow strong again with a little bit of you in my heart and body." And I remember my own release of tears and doubt when a strong blonde nurse, in pale blue, steadied my forearm and I heard or felt, "He's gone now. You can let go whenever you're ready."

I don't know if she said it with her voice or her eyes or if she only stood beside me and let me know. She was like some Norse spirit, there but not there, reassuring me that it's all just different phases, giving me permission to stay and to go. I held on to Daddy's thickly haired forearm, the arm usually covered in heart-pine sawdust curls from his woodworking.

He was a crusty, old-school, Lowcountry man who'd bellow like a bull at the mention of spirits or death doulas. He saw the world in black and white, right and wrong. His whole body would shudder, starting with his neck, when he saw a rat or heard a liberal talking. If, only if, he ever heard me say out loud in public anything about a Norse spirit, he'd do that same shudder. And if he heard me say something about how an armadillo spoke to me, he'd practically have a seizure, hang his head in confusion and a really long, loud sigh would as much as say, "Boy, an armadillo is a pest that digs up the yard. Get rid of it."

He knew the facts about armadillos, though—how they live in separate sex colonies, all the boys sleeping together all day, grubbing around at night, nose in duff, bumping into things, and rattling the leaves like wild horses. He respected them. He understood their nature. But when an armadillo got under the house and crushed the HVAC tubes, I would hear my father's voice, "Shoot 'im."

I did what I was told. But, after I did it, that injured armadillo, protected by his hide, went back to his brothers under the house. I crawled in to find him. He had huddled by a stack of rocks that helped hold the house up. That amazing creature said to me, "Just wait a few minutes now. You started it. Now, let me die in my own way. I'm saying goodbye to my brothers, but I'll come out soon." After pleading for privacy, he did as he told me, dragging his paralyzed body down the red dirt road. I just followed the trail. I dug his grave fast. So fast. But not fast enough to get him out of my mind. He forgave me, but I haven't forgiven myself yet.

I still see him now. Our faces just feet apart, under the low, old beams of the farmhouse. The ductwork he'd pulled down and shredded in between us. "Brother armadillo, here is my inadequate apology. I'm sorry. I know we caused this problem. I know you can't understand why we won't share our house, why I get to make the decision." I am trying to manage the balance of life and death on this little farm on this little dirt road, in this little moment.

I believe that my buddy Jay chose to die here on the farm. That conflicted young man who sought advice from Momma about his love deciding to change sexes, that angular, lanky man who wrenched stone, brick, and block into architecture, and who loved my end of things, too. He loved dirt and plants, the soft and the malleable. Jay came back to the farm to die. He was a man who didn't fit into most of this world, who really couldn't be soothed. That last day, a cold February day, we dug a thousand-foot trench and ended up coated in mud and exhausted. We didn't even clean up before our end-of-day ritual of sipping a beer while building a little fire. Later, we sat up late on the couch, looked at plans and sketches for new projects, and turned on *Game of Thrones*. A totally satisfying day. Comradery, achievement, plans—it was soothing to us both. The next morning, when I went downstairs to make our coffee, Jay was still on the couch. Stone cold.

Then today, just moments ago, when I walked out into the backyard, into the eye-searing August sunshine, I was hoping like crazy that the five-foot, bicep-thick rattler would just vanish. I told it: "Would you just go away, you beautiful creature? Go back to the swamp and do it fast. You can't be here." While I tried to think of other ways to get rid of this snake in the yard, all the memories of other deaths, other transitions ran through my head. "Does it have to be done? Does it have to be done by me? Does it have to be done now?"

While I was struggling with all of this, my seventy-eight-year-old mother stood beside me and read my mind. She answered the questions: "Shoot it! It's under my bird feeder! It might get under the clothesline or in the children's sand pile!" Momma, who would understand every word, every memory, and every prayer in this essay, loaded her .410-gauge shotgun and handed it to me. She read me and said, "No, I don't. I don't feel bad at all. But we'll do it this way. You take a shot, then I'll take a shot."

I killed today, and it brought all of these shards, these memories, to the surface.

At about 10 p.m., the creamy green flowers of night-blooming jasmine release their sweet candy fragrance.

Ladies of the Night

Sometimes I sleep on the back porch with the dog. I often end up stretched out on the porch swing, but Sweetiepie and I usually start out on the floor together. She smells of popcorn. I love that puppy popcorn smell. She seems to like my smell, too. Unfortunately, for these past few months of summer, it has been too miserably hot to sleep outside. But nights are cooling off now with the arrival of September. The air is getting a little drier, and Sweetiepie and I are back on the porch some nights. September also brings longer nights, coaxing a singular plant to its peak. Night-blooming jasmine's needle-sized green flowers go unnoticed in the daylight, but at night, those same unremarkable little flowers explode with a mysterious, delicious fragrance that I've always struggled to describe.

It's about 9:30 p.m., and I still have time before the air fills with perfume. Barefoot and with no flashlight, I walk all the way around the field to shut off irrigation valves. I've never stepped on a snake in the dark, but I have stepped on other things. Little thorny branches where Momma pruned and left rose stems in the path? Yes. American toads? Yes, a lot of them. A knot is the name for a group of toads. We have a sizable knot of toads living in this lily field, and one night an unlucky member from that knot got squished between my toes.

While I'm walking, there's no need to look down. My feet know the field. In fact, it's so dark that looking is pointless anyway. Feet and nose lead the way. There's an unmistakable feel of walking on old hay mulch that smells moldy. That feel and that smell mean I'm still in the flower fields. But at the edge, the fresh grass and uncut hay send up a dusty, lemony-sage fragrance. It's the base note. Other perfumes mingle into the smell of uncut hay. A powdery, Froot Loop cereal fragrance wafts in. It means a 'Jubilee' flower is opening up for nocturnal moths. A little later on the way back from the fields, that pungent fig smell tells me I'm getting close to the house again.

I've spent many nights on this porch. We used to have a beagle hound who'd run off at dusk, chasing whatever animal smell reached her nose. I'd sleep lightly, waiting for that roaming hound, hoping she'd find her way home whole, not torn up by a boar or coyote. Tonight is different. Tonight I have a loyal shepherd by my side, one who'd never roam and who offers her lovely puppy popcorn perfume. Tonight I'm waiting for another favorite fragrance, too.

At 10 p.m. sharp, little whiffs of the sweetness I've missed all year finally debut. Minutes later the fragrance floats in the air. It flows around the corner of the house, down the slope, under the magnolia tree, around the front porch, and into the road. On dry nights, it floats high, but by the end of the month, when the rain returns, the fragrance will stay low, hugging the ground like fog.

How to describe such an intoxicating fragrance? It smells like the first man I dated, who wore way too much Polo. No. Yes. It's like cotton candy at the fair. Wait. Maybe it's more like incense from the little Indian grocery toward town. It definitely isn't like any smell from the woods—not from our woods anyway. It's a foreign smell flowing down into the swamp, through the smooth black trunks, mingling in with my favorite smell— the scent I'd wear if I wore cologne and if it were a cologne—the smell of the yellow underbelly of the dark magnolia roots. That dark swamp is full of exotic fragrances. The fragrance filling the air now is a little bit of all of that. The base note of this night blooming jasmine is definitely PEZ. Take your pick—Mickey Mouse, Santa Claus, Miss Piggy, or Princes Leia. *Cestrum nocturnum* smells like a fresh pack of PEZ.

That candy smell overwhelms Sweetiepie's puppy smell. I wonder what she thinks it smells like? She's never had a PEZ. Maybe she thinks I'm making this smell. Other important questions come to mind, and I'm torn between giving in to the sensual fragrance or marveling at the mechanisms of this botanical release.

I read the 1955 dissertation by Roy Sachs, a Caltech student, who sniffed out the exact molecules and mechanisms to explain this awesome biological process. It goes something like this. All summer long, specialized cells in the plain-looking jasmine leaves act as a chemical clock. The leaves count the hours of dark each night, the nyctoperiod. Then they count the hours of light the next day. They keep track of the difference between dark and light minutes. When they notice two days in a row shorter than the nights on the heels of five days longer than nights, the clock in the leaves sends a signal to the growing tips and sets off an alarm. Then the jasmine's fragrance is released to flow over the porch swing, down the road, and into the swamp, eventually attracting moths from far and wide.

I finally give into the fragrance. No more words or analysis. I close my eyes and still my thoughts. Images of gardens shaped by September's shortening days float through my mind—I envision crispy khaki grass, glossy yellow magnolia leaves dropping from the tree, rusty golden pine straw. I see things getting ready for autumn and looking kind of dry. The falling leaves get crispy on the dusty driveway in September. It's OK. Those drying plants really need no irrigation, no solution from me. They will survive. The dry spell will end next month with the start of hurricane season. Dog days are waning, dry leaves falling, PEZ fragrance filling the evening air, Sweetiepie and me sleeping on the back porch—all announce summer's transition to fall.

Tyler

Working on a farm in the South in September builds character. Mornings are so humid that we're drenched by ten, and afternoons are Africa hot. To keep from building too much character, we have a few little techniques to make it through the day. We seek shade whenever possible. We bring extra shirts and shorts to change into after lunch. We use outside showers for quick cool-downs during our breaks.

Our farm crew changes this time of year. Work slows a bit. Interns often leave, and high school help cuts back their hours, showing up only for afternoon and Saturday work. These farm boys, the local fellas who remind me of me, keep me going. Over the past twenty years scores of them have worked side-by-side with me and grown from shy boys to amazing young men. Our farm may not be mechanized and efficient, but I'm proud to say that every teen who's grown up on this road has had a job here. Every single one of them.

Tyler and Jacob were two of those farm boys who loved living out in the country—both were sons of family friends, both drove trucks, and both were raised right. Both valued the history and responsibility of their pocket knives. With a comfortable swagger and a smile for everyone, Jacob was a little older and a good bit taller, and he knew everybody in town. Tyler was much the opposite—slim and shy, introspective, and intense. Tyler walked fast and always looked ahead. He was determined. He avoided silly conversations. He spoke succinctly and with authority.

Those two helped each other understand something pretty big about life and people. The traits each admired in the other could be taken on and incorporated into their own personhood. In short, they helped each other grow up.

For six or so years, Tyler sat at our break table. Break table is a euphemism for Momma's kitchen table. Interns and farm fellows don't so much work as get adopted here. Sometimes it's my goal to broaden their food world—have them try two new things each week. "A little kimchi with your PB&J? That's not a question. Try it."

Tyler knew what he liked. He did not need to try new kinds of cookies. He'd never even think of trying my favorite snack of cottage cheese and salsa. On the first day of work, he watched where Momma stored the Doritos, and for years after, he beelined it for that shelf.

He was the same in work. We butted heads a lot. Conversations often went like this:

Me: "Tyler, can you get a Facebook profile?"

Tyler: "No."

Me: "But it's so we can make a group for daily work, we share calendars, upcoming projects, notes, and even what tools we need. It'll make planning easier."

Tyler: "I don't want a Facebook page."

We never converted Tyler. He was set on Doritos and flip phones. As a career, he was set on metal work. As far as I know, he never considered professional gardening as a life's work any more than he considered sushi a main staple of his diet. Luckily, farm work and making gardens and growing lilies mean doing things with tractors, tools, and people—bush hogging, oil changing, building sheds, teaching visitors about rural life, and chasing donkeys. Tyler loved all those things, especially working with any piece of machinery.

One new thing that Tyler had to consider long and hard before accepting its utility was using layers of wood chips inoculated with mushrooms to build the soil. It's something we've done for years. Mushrooms recycle the chipped trees, turning them back into rich dirt. With some instruction, Tyler got it. He realized that frequent tilling kills the life in the soil and that a world of critters down there needs feeding. He spread wood chips and gently layered in the cardboard and the fungi spawn. Then when he came to work, he'd jump out of his old Ford truck, slam the heavy door, and go right to the spawn to see what was happening.

We're so proud of helping to change quiet boys into confident men. Men of independence. Men who question. Men who always say, "Yeah, we can do that." And men who know where and how they fit in and complement a team. Tyler never wanted to garden, but he told me once, "This is what old farms need to do to survive today—figure out new crops and be places for people to visit and places for learning." In spite of everything, Tyler took pride in his role on this lily farm.

Toward the beginning of summer, Tyler was planning to graduate from high school and looking forward to a real job, welding. He loved that, and I was happy for him. But what happened next—well, in my two decades of managing interns here on the farm, there has never been a bad time or rough patch to compare.

Suddenly Tyler just wasn't.

He died in a tragic car accident.

Having always used writing to express what's in my heart and to present my impressionist-like take on the world and gardens, I found myself unusually quiet. I was unable to write about Tyler's death. I couldn't figure out how to share the depth and the shattering. How do you write down a massive black hole in your heart? What's there to say? You just push the loss to a heavy corner and move one step at a time. That's what I've done.

Tom, Momma, young Jacob, and I worked through the summer. We mowed, dug bulbs, and boxed up and shipped packages like always, but work periods, breaks, and lunches were more quiet.

We've managed now that September is here. We finally talked about it some. Yet throughout the summer, I had felt torn between two contrasting constants—Tyler's death and Tyler's presence. A simple look or nod at some tool that he had loved could feel like an intimate conversation tugging on the heart.

I know he had lots of great men as role models in his family life. But there's something about independence from family, something about a job, that contributes to feeling like a man. I felt it in the '70s when I was a teen and as I grew confident, as I gained duties and respect, as I became part of the team on Mr. Frank Atkinson's farm. You get that you're OK, that you can grow and mold your own self. You go away to do that, away from family, and then come back home to love the earth, the barns, the woods, the people who shaped you. On your own terms.

We love our interns and all the hard work they do on the farm. These young people help us transform our farm while finding and building and transforming themselves. Honestly, though, when they leave in August or September, we kind of enjoy the quiet. But we're at a low point this time around. I don't have the words to say how low. I can't tell you how many ways I know Tyler would have made our life, our farm, our community better for the coming decades.

I comfort myself, and hopefully some of you, by remembering how Tyler became a man in front of our eyes. And he loved that newfound feeling of being comfortable in his own skin. He loved dirt, hay, mushrooms, and sunshine. He loved the satisfaction of caring for the farm and bringing beauty and nutrients from the earth. He'd certainly roll his eyes or ignore that sentence, but it's still true. He reveled in being a man, and he took pride in the accoutrements of farming. Every one of us, his family, and you who met him, can be proud of helping to have nourished those things that Tyler loved being.

WARM COLORS AND THE ROMANTIC FLOP OF PERENNIAL
GARDEN MUMS USHER IN OCTOBER.

Garden Mums and Matrons

Early on a cool morning, I'm over by the old outhouse, knee deep in a roiling row of golden mum flowers. Their color glows and the chrysanthemums' rich tones warm this chilly morning. During the summer, mum greenery sprawled over crinums and a row of St. Christopher lilies right up to the outhouse door. Then last week, the mum buds unfurled into pumpkin, rust, purple, and gold flowers, the colors of fall. All's quiet as the sun rises this morning. The owl that was hooting when I came out must have gone to bed, and the bees haven't woken up yet.

My morning task is to get through the mum sprawl and dig some lily bulbs now hidden below. With my boot, I gently part the golden mum froth, slide through the smelly thicket of stems, squat, and feel around for the neck of the bulbs. I finagle a small, sharp spade through the greenery, ease it into the ground, and retrieve bulbs without messing up the mums. Then I head to the washstand and back to the house for a coffee warm-up. By mid-morning, colors still glow but it's no longer quiet. The whole place is abuzz. As mum oils warm with fall sunshine, honey bees, wasps, flies, and hungry insects of all shapes congregate for an October feeding frenzy.

The scent of mums turns some people off. Camphorish and vegetable-like, the smell reminds people of florists and funerals, but I love it. I love that every single part of the plant has its own aroma. Early in the season, slowly creeping leaves go unnoticed except when I step on them and release their woodsy fragrance. Today the breeze must be carrying it pretty far to attract this insect crowd. I make a mental note to divide the plants in January. When I dig their roots in a few months, I'll get to enjoy their grapefruit-herbal smell mixed with the scents of cold dirt.

As October passes, mum petals will change colors. The flowers on the plant next to me right now started out creamy then turned white. By the end of the month, its petals will be purple like the top of a turnip. It reached five feet tall and has climbed a fence by the compost bin. Today, its flowers flop over like some out of season hydrangea.

I don't know its real name. Garden mums got their start in the '30s, but by the '50s their floppy habit had led to modern gardeners' disdain. Particular names got lost over the years, but gardeners who loved mums and ignored fashion trends kept them safe and passed them on to us. Today they have new names—found names like "Ryan's Rainbow" and "Judy's Yellow." That huge white mum by the compost pile is now called "Senate Street" in honor of the little garden where I found it growing in Columbia, South Carolina. Mum flowers with their October colors bring to mind old friends and gardeners I wish I'd known.

As the afternoon approaches, I head into town to ship the bulbs that have been packaged and to run some other errands. In town, I see the stark difference between those country mums and their city cousins that show up in stores in October. I call these city cousins "florist mums," and I feel sorry for them. Shorn like sheep, they sit on pallets out front of the Piggly Wiggly, waiting and hoping for a home, each trying to stand out in the crowd. A football-minded florist fixed these up. I'm sure of it. Orange-flowered mums sport shiny foil wrapping around their pots, each decorated with a tiger paw print. Bright-red-flowered ones in black foil have silky bulldog-print ribbons. A "Go Cocks" sticker, anchored by a plastic stick in the dirt, poked above the garnet blossoms of another little mum. I hope they all get taken home, because those left here on Monday morning will surely be tattered and pushed to the side by a pallet of pumpkins and a giant inflatable spider.

To my eye, these city mums just don't fit in on the farm. But every year, dutiful son that I am, I buy a few because Momma loves them so much. She'll bring home some from the discount rack, telling me "they might come back next year, you never know." She's right. They might. So I plant the sad, crusty-flowered, cast-off plants for her and think of other random things I used to have disdain for—Jello salads, *Eight is Enough,* jack-o'lantern garbage bags, young Justin Bieber. I still don't love any of those things, but I know even potted-up florist mums bring some people October joy.

Back on the farm, a late afternoon tour group takes selfies in the sea of golden garden mums that laps at the outhouse door. I tell them this field full of mums was bare six months ago and they can do something like this at their homes. They just need to pull little plugs from the mother mum and plant them around. It's how a few tiny plants of mums can become an acre of flowers by fall. And with everyone's attention focused, I can preach a little bit about organic pesticides that come from mums, how the roots till the soil for us, and how their flowers feed the bees.

I also tell them that just before dawn each morning, a hoot owl sits in the pecan tree, above the mums and outhouse. They usually don't get the import behind that statement and look a little puzzled. So I explain that for rabbits and rodents, the thicket of stems makes a perfect home. Their families grow throughout the summer. Then after the flowers feed the bees, after their colors fade, the mums make a rich hunting ground for our owl. I know October is passing as that old owl hoots more often and mum flowers fade to their final color, coffee brown.

Calm Before the Storm

Plants work for us. All year their roots till, bind, and add nutrients to soil that our lilies and veggies can use. Cool season cover crops like clover, oats, turnips, and arugula are our workhorses and germinate in October when we have warm soil and cool nights. Our work in the field includes prepping soil, sowing seed, and nursing tender seedlings through their early days. Success here helps guarantee the success of our crops for the next six months. I should focus completely on these tasks, but focus eludes me. There's also mulching to be done, leading tour groups, and trucking over to Georgia for a load of something or other. Then there's that hurricane pounding Puerto Rico and targeting our nearby coastal friends, their homes, their gardens, and their lives. There's a heaviness, a sense of dread of what might come. It's a combination of the not knowing and the fact that work, plans, and lives—all the things that we pre-

---

PLANTS THAT WORK FOR US, LIKE NITROGEN-FIXING HYACINTH BEANS,
SHINE IN THE GLORIOUS DAYS OF EARLY OCTOBER.

tend to have control over—may be completely thrown off track or brought to an end.

October afternoons can still reach 90°F, dehydrating and killing tiny seedlings. Sprinklers help. But—as much as we might hope the storm bypasses our coast, less than 200 miles from the farm—rains from that hurricane would be better, making seeds like clover swell up so their young white rootlets can pierce the seed coat and creep out. Clover roots drill down to find a dormant bacteria in endospore form, which is sort of like a seed itself. Down there in the dark, seed and endospore get it on and intertwine to become one thing—a symbiotic organism whose roots have little nodules where bacteria live. Together they pull free nitrogen from the air and turn it into fertilizer for our plants. They're efficient, awesome, microscopic fertilizer factories working away underground. They make us happy, and the fresh green mat of tiny clover leaves makes a delicious snack for the donkeys.

We plant more than clover. Different parts of the fields need different sorts of work from different cover crops. Turnips till the soil. Mustard roots release a gas that kills nematodes. Arugula shades out winter weeds. Larkspur and toadflax will, in spring, make lots of people smile. The fields become a patchwork quilt of cover crops. Getting the right combination requires an understanding of what's happened in each area during the previous year and what needs to happen in the year to come.

Some parts of the field do not get seeded with cover crops. Tons and tons of mulch-hay get rolled out during the fall. Some special rows, the ones that hold Christmas Crinum bulbs get bundled up with this fresh, fluffy hay to ensure that they look great for gifts. So there are seeded areas and areas covered in hay. There's something else in the patchwork, and it's related to our reluctance to let go of summer. We simply can't cut down the waning okra plants that still make a few pods. And the purple zinnias, even though they're covered with leaf spot, still look so pretty. Let's work around those.

Part summer and part winter, October is a patchy and turbulent month.

We don't really get full-on hurricanes here. But we always get serious tropical storms and remnants of hurricanes that give us days of rain and winds. So this time of year we find time to stop farming and do some prep work like pruning weak limbs, trenching around barns, and sharpening saws.

We try to coordinate seed sowing with the coming storms. This means that I usually try to get an extra area or two of seeds planted during stormy October evenings just before the thick, cloudy dark descends with its horizontal mist. Then around three in the morning or so, when I get woken up by the raging storm, I can take comfort in knowing that the section of the patchwork I got seeded will germinate uniformly and without interruption.

The morning after a storm brings with it a determined drive to get outside and see what has happened—to see proof of how tiny we are in comparison to Mother Nature and to see how much work is needed to get things back to normal. On one particular morning, the sun comes up, but the light is wrong. Its color is different. Instead of the low golden beams of a sunrise, green light fills the fields. It takes a minute to realize that the morning sun, normally rising over the horizon, is partially obscured, and tousled leaves are casting sideways shade.

A giant pecan tree went down last night, but it can wait. It's just one tree down for us and no other damage. Instead, we're heading to the coast. There's serious cleanup to do there, and people need help. Daddy made sure we always understood the importance of volunteering to help out friends, family, and strangers in need.

In 1989, the morning after Hurricane Hugo, Daddy along with me and a dozen other men headed out with a tractor trailer load of Kleenex. He'd gotten that donated and rounded up this team. We left the farm, just on the edge of the destruction zone, and showed up somewhere near Johns Island as the National Guard and the Red Cross set up—before anyone had a chance to close the whole coast off. I remember chainsawing with Daddy on top of a tarpaper-sided shotgun shack. A twenty-foot-round oak had literally split the house in two. We could see into the kitchen on one side of the trunk and into the bedroom on the other side. It was like looking into a doll house. The stout little lady who lived there still had propane, so she was cooking for people who were in greater need. We didn't know her. She kept calling up, offering coffee or breakfast: "More people worse than me. I'll cook all day." She called me "sir" every time she spoke to me even though she was a good sixty years older than I was. I like the word *sir* when it's a term of earned respect, a recognition of life lived and wisdom learned. But she called me "sir" as was the norm of her generation, because I was white. It made me feel tiny and self-conscious and exposed and ashamed.

That stuck with me. The lady of the doll house made me aware of my privilege. She touched on my need to change, to be part of a greater change.

Back on the farm after this recent storm, I find myself looking at the pecan tree lying on its side, and I think, "Your branch patterns stretched across two windows, your limbs like a giant black spider's legs against orange winter sunrises. Your leaves cast cooling shade on the picnic table where we had afternoon beers. Your pecans went into pies. Your history was shared with us by the old lady who planted you eighty years ago. And your truckloads of brown leaves—falling, mulching, breaking down, feeding the bacteria and clover seedlings—kept right on doing farm work while we were away. I'll miss you, sir.

EVEN IN NOVEMBER, PECAN LEAVES REMAIN ON THE TREES
WHILE NUTS RAIN DOWN POUNDS OF DELICIOUS PROTEIN.

Pecans and Hot Legs

I'm alone on this misty Sunday morning. With a dog. And a donkey. (Three donkeys, in fact.) And a cat. Every footstep lands on a nut that rolls, crunches, or conforms to my boot sole. I put two in one fist, then squeeze them with the other hand. There's a slow crack as one opens. Bitter brown corduroy stuff surrounds the golden meat. I snack. The other nut goes into my back pocket for later. Some guys have that Skoal ring in the back pocket of their jeans, the imprint of the tobacco tin they carry. In November, I have a pecan oval ring from the champion pecan that stays in my back pocket.

Even in the chilly mist, I'm compelled to pick up a bucketful. It's like one of those OCD things. Or like hoarding food. The process satisfies me down deep. The ethic of it satisfies me, too—dirt turns into plant, plant turns into food, and if I'm industrious, into cash. My sister, on the other hand, always despised picking up pecans. As teens, it was our fall income, selling pecans as well as turnips off the tailgate of the pickup. It was how we made our Christmas money. It was all way too dirty and country for her. I wonder about her. How could anyone not love squatting, pushing aside leaves, collecting the best nut in the world? When I'm picking up pecans, I'm close to the earth and my farm animals nuzzle my back. I'm gathering stuff that's just lying on the ground for someone else to turn into pecan pies.

I squat with a bucket in front of me and get into the rhythm. Brush away leaves, reach forward, pick, swing arms, and drop nuts in the bucket. It's like a dance. Good nuts hit the pail and sound solid, like a bass drum. Bad nuts sound hollow, like a snare drum. As a pecan hits the shed's tin roof and bounces down like a twangy Rod Stewart guitar riff, I listen to the music and the rhythm—the thud, thud, clack, clack, clack, thud. Then—Ka-pau! Bamalama, bamalama, boom bang!

Back in the '70s, my sister Weasa and I picked up pecans after school. We worked by the gallon: one gallon, one quarter. I could get twenty gallons, five dollars, of good nuts while she was complaining or while she spent half the afternoon trying to make the whole situation more exciting by setting up a music system. She'd go up to her bedroom, open the huge windows, and perch a three-foot speaker on the sill. We didn't have heat in the house, so it didn't matter if the windows were open on chilly days. She'd stack eight-track tapes—*Frampton Comes Alive!, Hotel California,* and good old Rod Stewart. His "Hot Legs" got lots of play during those November afternoons.

Because my sister was the DJ while we picked up pecans, she kept running upstairs to switch tapes. Remember that thud sound that eight-track players made between songs? It's not unlike the sound all those pecans made hitting my bucket while Weasa was busy with the music. All that prep and DJ time ate into her productivity. It was her idea and what she wanted to do, but since I also enjoyed the music and sang along, I should have given her part of my haul. At the end of the afternoon, though, I'd pour my unshared pounds of pecans onto the scales, then into the big communal bucket, and make a tally mark on the notebook Momma and Daddy kept to track our pay.

Just the other day, forty years later, we were picking up nuts together. Weasa's a teacher now and she had stopped by after school. While we were putting nuts in our buckets, I wondered if she'd finally found the serenity—the satisfaction—in picking up pecans. I wondered if she had finally understood that this work represents the ethic that built old-style American farms, turned earth and muscle into food, turned excess into sales, and turned our attention to nurturing the land for the next generation. So I asked her, seeking a deep conversation. She stood up, shuddered from her shoulders down, not unlike how Daddy would have done when he saw a rat, and said, "No, I hate it, every bit of it. But I love Momma's pecan pies in the freezer all year." Then she pulled out her phone and put on the new Rod Stewart, the Stardust duet album, and we went back to picking up pecans while Rod crooned.

I love Rod's rendition of "Way Back Home" when he sings about the values that make a family strong:

> *How can I ever thank you for the lessons*
> *that I've learnt*
> *And the precious warmth and comfort*
> *that I've felt at every turn...*
> *I will always find my way back,*
> *always find my way back home.*

The nostalgic ballad plays in my head on this misty Sunday morning. Moos and motorcycle noises travel across the fields. I'm still squatting, brushing leaves off the cooling autumn earth. I crack a nut, pick the meat out, and give half to that old donkey who's looking over my shoulder. The dog wants some, too. Even taking time to share a little with the animals, I still get five gallons in twenty minutes. I pour them into Momma's communal bucket. She'll smile later, when she and a few of her friends, the ladies' brigade, come out after church. They don't squat. Instead they use a variety of weapons, pecan picker-uppers of all sorts and designs. They pick up, sort, and cull, all the while planning for pecan pies, enjoying being together, and taking pride in being industrious. It's a social thing. Weasa will probably come and keep them company and talk about who's not here. The thought makes me laugh a little, makes me proud. I want the nostalgia and serenity of this November moment to last, but a few nuts bam down on the tin roof, the donkey brays, and the twangy guitar riff from "Hot Legs" suddenly screams in my head. Thanks, Sis. In Rod's words, "I love ya' honey."

Donkey's Work

Tell me about a time you've been caught outside naked.

It's a good conversation starter and usually ends in a good laugh. My response to that question is serious though. It happened on a chilly November night and explains how I fell in love with a fat old donkey named Buck.

We do all the work by hand on our little farm—no tractors, no plows, no weed-killers. We work hard, bending, sweating, climbing, and almost always clothed. Of course, we use all sorts of tools. Sometimes work animals are tools, too. Chickens make food, guineas eat ticks, cats catch rodents, and other animals actually get sold for income. There are no freeloaders and no roadside attraction animals here.

We used to have goats. They were a source of income for us. People from the local Mexican, Jamaican, and Arab communities would come buy them just before holidays.

BUCK BONDS WITH ME OVER A CUP OF COFFEE ON A
WARM NOVEMBER MORNING.

Because they aren't high maintenance, goats just took care of themselves. They didn't run away, and I knew how to give the required shots. It was a smart idea to have those goats. They ate the weeds, doing their share of work around the farm, until it was time to sell them.

Goats don't like the taste of crinum. That means we could let the goats into the crinum field. They'd eat only the weeds, not the crop. Donkeys are the same way. Both love nutsedge, which is a pernicious weed to us, although today nutsedge is sold in trendy organic stores as the high-protein superfood called tiger nuts. Apparently hipsters make expensive shakes with it. But for us, it's just a weed.

Buck the donkey likes it raw. That donkey mows it down. For a while, he was just a work animal, but after what I'll call the "naked night," Buck and I bonded. He became more than a weeder, and now we're deeply connected. Sometimes when I'm having a beer at the end of the day, he puts his head in my lap. Sometimes while we're working, he stretches his neck into a big *U* and waits for me to notice him. We lock eyes in a silent salute and nod, like the nod that guys give each other on the street. Buck doesn't understand why I collect his poo. I don't understand why he love-nips my bicep. We don't ask each other.

Buck does have one defect. He's an overachiever. And this is how I came to be outside naked at 3 o'clock in the middle of a chilly November night, drenched in sweat, heart pounding, protecting my last goat, Martha Brown.

A little backstory, first. We needed something to protect our goats from the coyotes. We had heard that donkeys supposedly love and protect goats and run off coyotes. To confirm this, we asked an expert, Miss Gail from down the dirt road. She had a herd of dwarf donkeys and said it was true that donkeys protect goats. She also told us that donkeys get lonely, so we'd need two. She surveyed her herd and spotted Buck and his lady friend called Precious Baby. Miss Gail loved them too much to let them go completely. But she decided she could loan them to us as long as she could visit them and if we'd call her when they had a baby.

Well, it turns out that she was right. Donkeys do have an innate hatred of four-legged canines. They kill coyotes and dogs, too. Shortly after taking the donkeys to the farm, I saw Buck chase a fit, young male lab until the dog was slobbering and shaking. That dog never tried to cut across Buck's pasture again.

As you may have gathered by now, the voracious coyotes in the area had discovered our goats. Our hearts were breaking. Our goats may have been weeders and a source of income, but like good farmers, we were their stewards. Also like good farmers, we had fallen in love with these animals.

Enter Buck, who took control of the pasture on his first day. His only job was to protect the goats, and he did it. The coyotes never came back. But Buck didn't distinguish between different types of bothersome little four-legged creatures. He ran coyotes, dogs, and goats out of his pasture. We tried to teach him to share at least a little corner of the pasture. But Buck was stubborn, and he chased them out, again and again. Like a swarm of bees, those goats went over the fence, right to the front porch. Goats do not like rain and the porch had chairs and things to climb on, so it made sense they felt safe and at home there. But there was only one problem. The coyotes picked them off one by one from the porch.

For a while the coyotes wouldn't attack the biggest and last goat, Martha Brown. She'd eat the hydrangeas in the yard during the day, then hoof it up to the front porch at dusk. She took to standing on an old church pew that we had on the porch, peering into the living room window to watch *Wheel of Fortune* over Momma's shoulder. She was part of the family.

Then on that November night, the howling of a pack of coyotes woke me up. It was like a soundtrack from a Dracula movie. Those coyotes were around the porch and ganging up on her. I jumped out of bed, ran downstairs, and out the front door, past Martha Brown's church pew, where I saw her speeding by. Three coyotes zoomed past, closing the gap, right on her black heels. I jumped in and started to chase them, waving my arms and howling. I kind of doubt this terrified the coyotes, but it must have at least startled them or made them wonder what the heck this was behind them. We ran in a giant circle around the house. Tom came down. He was both confused and afraid that the coyotes would turn and get me. Momma showed up in her nightgown, probably with a shotgun.

With an audience then, I was just doing my job, protecting my goat. Buck's job actually. Buck had joined the audience by this time and was standing in the darkness behind the fence of his pasture. Finally the coyotes left in total confusion. He had my back. Buck gave a solid, affirming bray, just so I knew that he knew we were still good—even though I sometimes do things like run around the house naked in the middle of the night. There are some things donkeys just don't understand and don't ask about.

A HANDFUL OF REINDEER MOSS IS LIKE HOLDING BUBBLES.

Gumdrop Tree Trek

This time of year, I can easily spot mayhaw trees, even mixed in with all sorts of other bare-branched trees. Mayhaws have a few fruits still hanging on their branches, like tiny burgundy apples. And lots of thorns. The thorns make mayhaws distinctive among the winter silhouettes of the woodline. Some have bigger, sharper thorns than others. It's the thorns that make mayhaws important in December, when we have a special use for those wooden barbs. The bigger the mayhaw thorns, the more sparkly, glittery, delicious-looking, and magical the Christmas treat we make every year—a rainbow-colored, candy-laden, gumdrop tree.

"Let's go get the haw branches and make a gumdrop tree!" That was the bait each December. Once we kids were hooked, my grandfather guided us into the woods. Through the windbreaks, the meadow, and pine forest to an open glade with its bumpy carpet of reindeer moss and a few scraggly haws. The adventure of the hike and promise of lots of candy made it a fun trip. But I suspect for him then, like me now, making gumdrop trees had more to do with passing on a love for nature, for winter woods, for moss and mayhaw.

I never really plan this. It just happens during some lull in December work on a day there are children around, who need to get out of the house. On the way to the glade, the tree canopy changes from towering pines to thirty-foot sassafras, persimmon, and mayhaw trees. A few more steps and suddenly everything opens up, and the groundcover changes. A carpet of reindeer moss dominates. Only a few bronze grasses live in the seafoam expanse of moss. Way out in the middle of the reindeer moss, there's a little island of shrubs. On that island grow two stunted, ten-foot mayhaw trees. Something keeps them dwarf and gnarly and their thorns close together. The density of thorns makes those branches perfect for our Christmas gumdrop trees. With an artistic eye, shiny spray paint, and bags of sugared candy, we'll turn these wicked thorns into joyful, sparkling, rainbow gumdrop trees.

Today I have three young cousins joining me for their first mayhaw-gathering experience, so I'm stoked. I get to be a teacher, and I get to pass on the secret of this special place. I tell the boys to look around and notice how big the trees grow at the edge of the woods. "This glade is kind of like a pond. The moss is like the water. Look closely and you can see that it even looks like bubbles in the water. Sweet bubbles, too. If you're ever lost in the woods, you can eat it. Seriously, y'all try some."

The youngest, most mischievous, cousin locks eyes with me and does it. He takes a big bite. His reaction lets me know he's going to play along, not letting on that the moss has turned to a yucky soft sand in his mouth. He tells the others that it's good and sweet. They follow his lead but immediately start spitting fast and furiously, dancing around. Realizing it's a trick, they all tackle the little perpetrator, who's a regular Huck Finn in hundred-dollar neon sneakers. He's likable, a leader. But when I ask if he wants to go to wildlife camp, he says, "No sir. I'd miss my Momma too much." I melt.

The boys horse around and grab handfuls of moss, putting it on each others' heads and taking selfies. Everybody loves this stuff (not to eat, of course). It's outside our normal way of seeing the world—neither solid nor liquid, neither plant nor animal, neither alive nor dead. It's squishy but resilient. Big but weightless. It reminds me of syllabub, that sweet dessert served in a glass, filled with sugary bubbles.

I figure since the boys are so engaged, I can get in one more lesson. "Hey, why do y'all think there are no real trees here? Why are these two little haw trees stunted? The reason is that this moss has a secret super power. It excretes a chemical that keeps seeds from germinating and makes trees grow poorly. It's protecting itself from being shaded out."

No one is impressed. We brought along saws, and they're ready to use them.

I hand these city boys razor-sharp Japanese pruning saws, and they launch into cutting the branches. Maybe I should worry about the kids with these saws. Instead, I tell myself to relax, that the tools are half the fun. Then I lean back onto a bed of moss. I feel the rays of the winter sun slice through the chilly air and enjoy their warmth on my face. My mind wanders off to fuzzy memories of some children's Christmas storybook. An adventure into the snowy woods, a bunch of children excited to trek into the woods and find the perfect Christmas tree to chop down with their double-headed axe. In that story, those children drag the Christmas tree home and decorate it with popcorn and candles. What we're doing right now is the southern version of that. If it were a children's book, it might be called *Mayhaws, Reindeer Moss, Sharp Saws, and Sugary Treats.* As the kids finish up, we drag the mayhaw branches back through the piney woods, under the live-oak tunnel and down the dirt road to the farm.

Back home, we drill holes into pieces of old barn wood and whittle mayhaw branches to fit in. The children like using the drill and knives. They like spray painting the branches silver and standing them up to replicate the thorny trees in the glade. Gumdrops go on each thorn. Discussion turns to finding out what my cousins learned today. That littlest of cousins, the prankster that he is, says matter-of-factly, "Nothing special." Then with a super-excited voice, "Hey, Jenks, can you tell us more about these gummy bears with sugar on them?" I roll my eyes, bellowing in a hilariously annoyed tone, "After all those great plant lessons, the only thing you really want to know about is candy? *Candy?*"

The hike to collect thorny old mayhaw branches means it's December. Almost Christmas. But it's deeper than that. This adventure means time is passing—not just the month, but the decades. I hope these boys remember this winter walk just like I remember December walks with Grangran. He knew that walking in the woods helped children learn plant names and nature lessons. But he also knew there were more important lessons to learn and carry for a lifetime. Stewardship. Searching out the most wicked thorns, eating a little bit of sandy moss, and making sparkly gumdrop trees build lifetime connections.

CAROLINE TURNS MAYHAW BRANCHES INTO A
GUMDROP TREE.

A Farm Beyond Us

Physical work in December revolves around two things: winterizing and packing gift boxes. The first includes tasks like wrapping pipes, mulching fields, and moving baby crinum and tender plants into the pit greenhouse. The second includes wrapping gift boxes and writing notes for Christmas Crinum gifts. But there's a more cerebral, difficult type of work, too—planning what business-minded friends call a succession policy for the lily farm. December is a time for reflection and thinking about the future.

Greenhouse work is more fun. We designed our greenhouse with help from a permaculture friend to utilize the earth's warmth and sunlight as primary heat sources. It's a small room, dug down three feet into the soil. Being inside is sort of like being in some kid's fort, sunken, surrounded by earth, and partially hidden from people outside. Big barrels of water sunken in the floor collect heat since the ground temperature is a constant

WE NEVER IMAGINED THERE WOULD HAVE BEEN A DESIRE TO GIVE BULBS AS GIFTS. HOWEVER, TODAY WE DIG AND SHIP CRINUM CHRISTMAS GIFTS.

fifty-nine degrees Fahrenheit. One thick red adobe wall forms the back and acts as a heat sink. Other walls, all of them glass, look out onto a small black pond. That water surface reflects sunlight through the glass for extra heat and light. All of those things contribute to keeping the space, the plants, and us warm.

In the beginning of December, I come in here to escape the cold and stay busy piddling, weeding, and watching over those baby crinum. Other plants winter over here, too. Momma's angel wing begonias and aloe cuttings tend to sneak into where some crinums should be. A dragon fruit cutting lies across the table like a chilly snake. While we're working in here, we're also thinking about plants that haven't come inside yet. We take stock of our tender plants. "Did we get the coleus cuttings? Where's that clivia, the one we grew from seed on Mao's tomb? How about the purple jade vines? They'll die out there."

On a cold December morning, the African bulbs, a Chinese begonia, and the Carolina mutt that I am snuggle together in this pit dug into American soil. We feel grounded and at home. This is a good time to take stock in other ways, too. I think about the cycles of farms. Ever since Europeans took over this bit of land, there have been boom and bust cycles including cotton, hay, and soybeans. The place was in ruins in the '70s. My parents brought it back. They had day jobs but managed to keep cows and chickens and grow our veggies. The farm was a hobby. When I came back with dreams of a new crop of lilies, I jumped into the daily grind of fixing it all up again. Looking ahead, I'd like to think we're going to break the boom and bust cycle. I like to think we're creating something that will last longer and be more connected to the earth. Even after I'm gone.

There is no succession policy. I have vague dreams about what might happen after me, after crinums. Could this become a little farming commune? Or maybe turn into some sort of nonprofit? Maybe a nephew or a cousin will come home and lead it into some new life. Or my young energetic friends from Mexico could take over. Maybe there's a future I can't imagine, a way to keep it going that I can't see. Even if I had a plan, I don't have complete control. This is a family farm, and we make decisions about the future together. I struggle with wanting to have a plan and not wanting to admit that one is needed. December, with family around, seems like a good time to wrestle with these questions. But none of us likes to think about growing old, needing help, or admitting that the place may fall back into disrepair. We focus on happy memories and on Christmas Crinum gifts.

It was a brilliant business idea. Christmas Crinum gifts bring in plant sales at a time of year when people are not normally gardening. But there was no long-term plan for this. In fact, the whole idea came from a road trip to Mexico and one particular night in a town called Tequila, during the December Feast of the Virgin of Guadalupe. Eleven bucks for the room included a crazy parade right under our paneless window. Marching Mariachi quartets, drag queens, and papier-mâché Catholic saints paraded in the street until the early hours of the morning. Cowboys shot off guns on the hour. All night. Every hour. Roosters crowed in confused response. On the hour. Every hour. At dawn a swarm of old men in dress pants swept the debris away and set up for day vendors, including guys selling some very nice mezcal and tequila. It was a crazy experience and one that I was sure would make for a magical, mesmerizing story.

Back on the farm, sitting around a bonfire with tequila, I started to share my tale. One of my inattentive friends kept interrupting, "Jenks, you know how they sell amaryllis this time of year, you should sell "Christmas Crinum!" Maybe he'd had a little too much agave juice. And luckily, lots of campfire brainstorming goes up in smoke. But his idea got me thinking. We ran with it. We figured out packaging and sent press releases to local newspapers. The name Christmas Crinum was just weird enough to grab people's attention. The quirky idea of sending a massive bulb and roots with sparkly wrapping and spiffy cards caught on. Tom got the wrapping and note writing down pat. First local papers featured the unique gift idea, then some blogs down on the coast. Eventually our Christmas Crinum caught the eye of a high-end glossy magazine editor, who put it in a gift guide called "Best Gifts from the South." We sent a box of bare bulbs to be photographed in New York City. That photographer sprawled our bulbs out on red silk, making them look all sexy and beautiful. That image of those country crinum bulbs as a sexy centerfold, on the pages of a glossy magazine, tickles me to no end.

Another image warms me, too—that of someone opening a box that releases the smell of dirt, feeling in the wrapping paper a mass of earthy roots, and being transported to a memory of their grandmother, some special little farm, or a day in the country. These connections define us. Whether we reject or embrace it, we are where we came from, and our stories define us. And most of us have a connection to rural America. All of us have a dependence on healthy dirt and farms. We need little reminders of this in everyday life.

This is where the hands-on daily grind of farm work and the more philosophical endeavor of long-term planning intersect. Planning for the future is based in the past. What do we want this to be? What do we want it not to be? December, a month of nostalgia and family and friends, is perfect for these reflections. My long-term plan may not seem like a plan at all. I want our little farm to be set up today so that the next generation can find inspiration in some unplanned road trip, some storytelling around a campfire, and a little history, but mostly so the next generation has enough of a connection to want to turn this farm, this world, into something we haven't even dreamed.

Epilogue

As the train pulled away with me on it, I saw through a yellowed double-pane window my parents slumped against each other, growing smaller on a dreary platform in London's Victoria Station. Looming larger, in my mind's eye, I saw African adventures, independence, freedom from country farms and family. This train was part of a transfer between flights, in the middle of my first airplane trip ever, twenty-two hours from the Lowcountry of South Carolina to the high plains of central Africa. My parents and sister had come along to London to see me off. John Denver whispered in my ear; "I'm leaving on a jet plane. Don't know when I'll be back again."

I was enrolled in the University of Zambia. I had an open-ended ticket, a 1979 copy of the Lonely Planet guide, and an untethered future. Africa enchanted me—so much that I dropped out of university and put that guidebook to good use. I found real freedom and self-reliance as I backpacked south into Zimbabwe.

I traveled alone but always ended up meeting other wanderers on the road. One day, downstream from Victoria Falls, I found myself with three intriguing offers from three intriguing travelers. Three different men at three different ages and stages of life. The ancient, intrepid British botany professor offered to take me into otherwise inaccessible forest in Zimbabwe. The handsome young Aussie backpacker in a once-posh hotel confused me by asking me to go camping far off the beaten path while seeming compelled to assert his heterosexuallity by insisting that we sleep head to toe: "You'd rather sleep with my feet near your face?" And I just smiled a lot at the middle-aged German hippy as he proposed sort of a job—to drive his jeep 800 miles to Pretoria where it needed new tires and work. An unimagined, exhilarating future to be sure. "I've friends along the way who will put you up," he said. "When you get into each little town, just ask where the happy Germans live. Take the jeep. No need for a map. One road. Kind of. Find your way, it's all an adventure." He said he'd found his elephant out there, and he wanted me to find mine.

I considered each of their offers for adventure. But I began to see something deeper. Each of these men seemed rootless—just what I'd wanted at one point. At this moment, though, I realized I kind of liked my roots.

So the next day at dawn I was sitting on a bus bench by a seemingly endless asphalt road. I was finally heading home.

With the mist of Victoria Falls rising behind me, I could hear the thundering cascade and the swoosh of flaming hot-air balloon burners. Tourists go up a few hundred feet or so, tied by thick ropes, to watch the sunrise over the falls. If anyone in a balloon had looked over this way, they wouldn't have noticed me waiting on a plain, trashy bank of compacted dirt that had been trodden down by fishermen and people walking to work. The river's so wide here you can't see the bank on the other side, just a spread of blue with some green, marshy rocks. The water is surprisingly slow-moving, given the tempest just down stream. But up-bank lay a brown, dusty, thorny world with wind-blown plastic bags quivering in the bushes and me perched on a white, wooden bench near a shack called The Oasis.

The public bus stops at The Oasis. It's the last chance to buy a pouch of water or a bag of parched peanuts before hours and hours of bumps across the desert. I was the only white guy, the only culturally inappropriate person wearing shorts, and one of the few male passengers without a goat. I did have a souvenir, a tiny stool/drum covered in goat skin, strapped on my backpack. For all those reasons, every man on the bus wanted to chat me up. It seemed that these incredibly poor, gentle, generous guys wanted nothing more than to hear about my world and invite me to their home for tea. I'd done that. A lot. It was fun at first. But by now, I'd realized people are people. There's always someone richer, someone poorer, someone working harder, and someone who wants you to marry his sister. I'd realized I missed my own people, our routines, our farm, and I wanted to explore our country. Those are tough, personal topics that don't make great bus-stop chitchat.

After a twelve-hour ride on the sweaty public bus with my knapsack and sort of a plan, I was sitting in the darkened Lusaka airport, waiting out the daily power outage. Eventually, I walked up the ramp into a massive British Air jet.

It was snowing in London when I arrived at dawn in a short-sleeved shirt and stepped right back on that cold gray train platform. What I saw now, in my mind's eye, was the memory of Momma crumpled, crying but letting me leave. Letting me roam into that unimagined future. Praying I'd come back.

I made it to the farm that year in time for Christmas. But it took fifteen more years to know I had truly come back home. To commit to it. It took helping Daddy die. Telling him I'd take care of things. It took gaining insight into myself. Like the German hippy counseled me to do, I had to find my way. I had to understand and be OK with the fact that a life of adventure or a conventional career wasn't my dharma. Neither satisfied me. I'm at home in the rootedness of the day-to-day routines of caring for growing things and the simple moments with family, dogs, and lilies.

I'm at home on this funky little flower farm. I'm at home and happy that it looks like an old country farm, yet isn't weighed down by all the destruction and oppression associated with small farms of the past. I'm at home and proud of this little farm's new ethos and commitment to nurturing life. I'm at home and hopeful that this little farm will remain a place committed to welcoming and connecting people to the earth and to each other.

I feel part of the earth here on the farm. That's an almost unbelievable statement to the ears of the younger me. But, yeah, it's true. I feel connected here. Kind of like a tourist in a hot air balloon over Victoria Falls. Tethered. But with a knife.

Index of Plant Names

A more complete index is available on jenksfarmer.com

General Index

Made in the USA
Columbia, SC
28 October 2021